D0589092

Contents

PART THREE

CRITICAL APPROACHES

PART FOUR

EXTENDED COMMENTARIES

PART ONE

INTRODUCTION

HOW TO STUDY A POEM

Studying on your own requires self-discipline and a carefully thought-out work plan in order to be effective.

- Poetry is the most challenging kind of literary writing. In your first reading you may well not understand what the poem is about. Don't jump too swiftly to any conclusions about the poem's meaning.
- Read the poem many times, including out loud. After the second or third reading, write down any features you find interesting or unusual.
- What is the poem's tone of voice? What is the poem's mood?
- Does the poem have an argument? Is it descriptive?
- Is the poet writing in his or her own voice? Might he or she be using a persona or mask?
- Is there anything special about the kind of language the poet has chosen? Which words stand out? Why?
- What elements are repeated? Consider alliteration, assonance, rhyme, rhythm, metaphor and ideas.
- What might the poem's images suggest or symbolise?
- What might be significant about the way the poem is arranged in lines? Is there a regular pattern of lines? Does the grammar coincide with the ending of the lines or does it 'run over'? What is the effect of this?
- Do not consider the poem in isolation. Can you compare and contrast the poem with any other work by the same poet or with any other poem that deals with the same theme?
- What do you think the poem is about?
- Every argument you make about the poem must be backed up with details and quotations that explore its language and organisation.
- Always express your ideas in your own words.

This York Note offers an introduction to the poetry of Emily Dickinson, *The Complete Poems* and cannot substitute for close reading of the text and the study of secondary sources.

Emily Dickinson published few poems during her lifetime. This was in part because of her own ambivalence concerning publication, something she simultaneously desired and yet described as being as 'foreign to my thought, as Firmament to Fin' (Richard B. Sewall, *The Life of Emily Dickinson*, p. 553). It was also, however, because her poems were, stylistically, so puzzling to her contemporaries, so strikingly unconventional and challenging. In 1862 Emily Dickinson sent four poems to the literary critic Thomas Wentworth Higginson along with a letter in which she asked: 'Are you too deeply occupied to say if my Verse is alive?' (Sewall, p. 541). Higginson advised her to delay publication: he thought the poems were disorderly and uncontrolled, the **metres** unruly, the **rhymes** careless, the syntax strained, the **metaphors** perplexing. He simply did not understand Dickinson's subtle and innovative stylistic effects. As many more recent critics have observed, Dickinson *is* a disturbing, even a dislocating, poet. Take a quick look at some of her opening lines to see that she still has this power to unsettle her reader. She might begin with some outrageous claim presented in a casual offhand manner, 'I like a look of Agony' (241), or 'I heard a Fly buzz – when I died –' (465); she might turn an accepted notion on its head, 'I dreaded that first Robin, so' (348); she might offer us what seems to be perplexing **paradox**, 'Success is counted sweetest / By those who ne'er succeed' (67), or a preposterous **analogy**, 'My Life had stood – a Loaded Gun –' (754); she might even jump out of the page to confront the reader: 'I'm Nobody! Who are you? / Are you – Nobody – Too?' (288). These opening lines might be disconcerting, sometimes shocking, sometimes bewildering, but they are also intriguing, and seductive. We want to read on to find out *why* she likes a look of agony, or *how* her life can possibly be like a loaded gun.

Looking back now, we can see that Emily Dickinson revolutionised poetry. She did this not by simply discarding all the received conventions of poetry at the time, but by taking these conventions and twisting them, undercutting them, making them work to her advantage. Her stylistic innovations challenge and disrupt the accepted conventions, in many ways anticipating what would be done in the twentieth century. For example, most of her poems are written in the **common** or ballad **metre**, that can easily sound monotonous and banal. Dickinson continually, however, breaks up the flow by introducing irregularities, by using such things as dashes which insist on pauses and upset the regular rhythm, or run-on lines which speed up the pace. She might allow the regular metre to dominate for a while in order to create a sense of peacefulness, and then disrupt it, break up the flow in order to enact some moment of agitation, in order to suggest a change in tone, a loss of calm or harmony.

Similarly, while she uses rhyme to create patterning effects and link **stanzas**, or ideas, to produce particular sound effects, she might disrupt her patterns, move from **exact rhyme** to **slant rhyme** or no rhyme. She makes rhyme work for her to become a tool she can use to disturb and dislocate.

Dickinson's language shares the same unsettling quality that we find in her manipulation of technical effects. She makes all things strange and new; her language makes us see common ordinary things and events in surprising and revealing ways. To say, for example, that 'The Soul has Bandaged moments –' (512) initially seems odd. How can something as abstract as a soul be submitted to something as concrete as bandaging? However, the description in fact beautifully captures the sense of limitation and constraint she is attempting to convey. Dickinson is notable for the compressed effects she achieves with her language. Frequently, we are forced to fill in the gaps in order to make sense of what she is saying. At other times we might find there are what have been called 'unrecoverable deletions', that Dickinson simply does not tell us what the connection between certain images or ideas might be. Her compressed language, the deletion of anything extraneous, often increases ambiguity and allows for a multiplicity of meaning. Sometimes, we are forced to confront the fact that Dickinson sometimes simply eludes all our attempts to pin her down, confounds our efforts to assign any one particular meaning to a poem. Dickinson's poetry strenuously resists both paraphrase and **closure**. She invites a multiplicity of possible causes, of possible readings: she invites us to fill out the meaning of her poems.

'Emily Dickinson is a great tease', as Karl Keller has aptly put it. Both her life and her poetry, he says, seduce 'without offering complete satisfaction' (*The Only Kangaroo Among the Beauty: Emily Dickinson and America*, p. 2). We know about her life and what often seems to be her rather eccentric behaviour in both small and large matters: the fact, for example, that she always wore white, or her decision to withdraw from the world and decline all visitors, even close friends. What we do not know is *why* she did so many of the things she did. All we can do is speculate – and there has been much sensational, and meaningless, speculation.

Dickinson, called 'the myth' of Amherst even during her own lifetime, has variously been constructed by her biographers and critics as the half-mad recluse, the New England nun, the morbid spinster obsessed by death, and the victim of a frustrated passion.

As a lyric poet, Dickinson is primarily concerned with the interior world, with abstract concepts, inner experiences, thoughts and feelings. She conveys these abstract ideas, however, in a highly concrete and visual manner. Her poems frequently proceed with the speaker trying to find similarities or differences in concrete physical experience for an experience which is interior and abstract, to describe those things which cannot be known through the senses by way of the senses. In '"Hope" is the thing with feathers –' (254), for example, she skilfully captures the essence of 'hope' by describing it in terms of a bird. But her definitions of the nature of interior experiences, of feelings and emotions, are frequently complicated by some lingering **ambiguity** concerning the nature of the abstract thing that she is trying to convey to us. There is an 'it' that she describes, but while we may have, by the end of the poem, a very full picture of what that 'it' feels like, what it resembles and what it is unlike, and what effect it has on her speaker, what 'it' is essentially remains unidentifiable. Again, we are left with a full sense of the effects that 'it' has, but are left unsure about the identity of the thing that causes these effects. In 'It was not Death, for I stood up' (510), for example, although we are given many concrete descriptions of what 'it' is not like – not death, not night, not frost, not fire, and what 'it' is like, at the end we are still not able to say with much confidence what 'it' is; we are, however, familiar with what it feels like. Here, as in many other of her so-called poems of definition, Dickinson attempts to describe a feeling, a psychic experience, with the use of concrete analogies drawing upon objects and things from the sensually apprehensible world. The descriptions are so suggestive that we can understand the feelings, even though, like Dickinson herself, we might not be able to put a specific name to them or identify what caused them: to do so would seem limiting and reductive.

Emily Dickinson's poetry cannot be called easy: she is disturbing; she disrupts conventions; she challenges our ways of seeing things and makes us see them anew; she jolts us out of any secure and comfortable position we may attempt to take, undercuts and frustrates our desire to find clear-cut explanations or closure. And, she makes us work. The reader of a Dickinson poem certainly cannot just sit back passively; the reader always has to play an active role. In a brief lyric (1212) Dickinson once commented

> A word is dead
> When it is said,
> Some say.
>
> I say it just
> Begins to live
> That day.

This is certainly true of her words, and of her poems more generally: as we read them and seek to understand what she might be trying to convey to us, they begin to live.

PART TWO

COMMENTARIES

Emily Dickinson (1830–86) wrote 1,775 short lyrics, only ten of which were published during her lifetime. She arranged her poems into groups, stitched them up into packets – sometimes known as the 'fascicles' – and accumulated them in a bureau drawer. When the poems were discovered after Dickinson's death, the task of editing and collecting them was given to a family friend, the writer and lecturer Mabel Loomis Todd, and to Thomas Wentworth Higginson, with whom Dickinson had corresponded for many years. In 1890 a selection of 115 poems appeared, *Poems by Emily Dickinson*. The volume was a great success and *Poems by Emily Dickinson, Second Series* followed in 1891. A third volume, edited by Todd alone, appeared in 1896. The poems in these three volumes had been significantly edited. The rhymes had been smoothed, the metre regularised, and words and metaphors replaced to make them, as the editors thought, more 'sensible'. Other editions followed over the years, but the Dickinson manuscripts did not become available for examination to anyone outside the circle of family and friends until the 1950s. The complete poems were first published in 1955 by Thomas H. Johnson in *The Poems of Emily Dickinson*. This was a variorum edition, that is, an edition which reproduces all the variations of any one text, containing all 1,775 poems. Dickinson's own punctuation, metre, rhyme and language were now restored. The text used in compiling these Notes is the Faber & Faber edition of *The Complete Poems of Emily Dickinson*, edited by Thomas H. Johnson (1970), which reproduces this 1955 variorum edition but presents only one form of each poem and omits the critical apparatus of the variorum. The poems we now read are Dickinson's and not the early edited versions; however, since Dickinson never prepared her poems as copy for the printer, the texts cannot be called 'final'. There is still much debate concerning the way they should be presented: many textual critics, for example, argue that the stanzaic forms into which the poems are placed cannot always be confidently seen as accurate on the basis of the handwritten texts. The poems, to which Dickinson did not give titles, are identified here by the numbers assigned in *The Complete Poems* and by their first lines. Following Johnson, the first date given is that conjectured for the earliest known manuscript and the date in parenthesis is that of first publication. The poems chosen for discussion here should provide an indication of the range of Dickinson's themes, voices and poetic techniques.

DETAILED COMMENTARIES

67 SUCCESS IS COUNTED SWEETEST 1859 (1878)

We most desire and appreciate those things we are denied

To understand the nature of something precious, like success, we must need and desire it intensely. Those who triumph in battle never understand the concept of victory as well as those who are defeated.

The first **stanza** falls into two parts: the first two lines offer an abstract proposition about success: it is sweetest to those who never attain it; the last two lines offer an explanation of this proposition: to understand how precious something might be, we have to desire, to need it, intensely. The second and third stanzas link together to offer a specific and concrete example of the general proposition put forward in the first stanza: those who win in battle never understand victory as well as those who are defeated.

This short **lyric** is a model of economy and effective organisation of thought. The first stanza is tightly knit together with the use of the **alliterative** 's' and 'n', and this alliteration along with the **end stopped** lines, emphasise the almost **epigrammatic** nature of the thoughts expressed. Although it is an abstract idea that is being summarised, the use of the image of 'nectar' to describe what is desired provides this abstract idea with a concrete and sensory form. The linking of stanzas two and three is emphasised by the use of **enjambment**; this encourages a build up of speed, helped by the presence of **slant** rather than **exact rhyme** in stanza two, which undermines the potential sense of **closure** at the end of the lines. The sense of speed and movement is then abruptly terminated in stanza three with the heavy thudding repetition of the alliterative 'd', the pauses emphasised by the use of the dash in 'defeated – dying –', and the return to exact rhyme at the end of the poem, which suggests finality.

But although there is in one sense a link between stanzas two and three, which combine to offer the specific example of the general proposition in stanza one, there is also a significant distinction made between stanzas two and three which justifies the division of the poem into three rather than two parts. This is the distinction between the many and the one. Why should the triumphant army be described as the 'purple Host'? Purple, traditionally the colour of the Roman emperor's robes, is a colour associated with power and dignity, and consequently appropriate to those who triumph, or, as Dickinson **metonymically** puts it, those who 'took the Flag'. Host is an archaic word for army, but it also suggests a great number, a multitude, and this emphasises the way in which Dickinson contrasts the triumphant many, in stanza two, with the defeated one, in stanza three. Instead of referring to the whole defeated army, Dickinson focuses in upon one individual, and the overall movement of the poem consequently progresses from the very general and abstract to the highly concrete and specific, from an abstract proposition to the feelings of one particular individual. Is it possible that in some way Dickinson is arguing for the superiority of defeat and frustration over victory and satisfaction? It is, after all, the dying soldier who comprehends the nature of success, who has won an increased awareness; the victors may have success, but they do not comprehend its nature.

nectar fluid produced in flowers and collected by insects; more generally, anything very sweet and pleasant; in Greek mythology, the drink of the gods

Host (archaic) army

199 I 'M 'WIFE' – I'VE FINISHED THAT –   1860 (1890)

The effects of marriage on women

A wife contemplates what she has gained and lost through marriage. She compares the state of girlhood with that of wifehood.

The speaker announces that she has become a wife and left behind her girlhood. She now feels that she has somehow changed and become a 'Woman', and compares herself to those in heaven looking back at the earth they have left behind. In the final stanza she stops herself making the comparison between girlhood and wifehood; all that is important, she claims, is that she is now 'wife'.

The speaker in this poem equates the word 'wife' with the words 'Czar' and 'Woman' to suggest that the role of wife bestows some privilege, recognition and maturity upon her. She initially seems calm and confident in her new position, and there is a hint of dismissiveness in the repetition of the word 'that' when she refers to the state of girlhood she has left behind. But what is the effect of the final line in the first stanza? Why should it be 'safer so', and does this suggest that while it may be safer to be a wife it may not necessarily be as preferable as she insists? There may be an implied qualification here that she prefers not to pursue. This could also be suggested by the placement of the dashes. In the first stanza they constantly break up the train of thought, perhaps suggesting hesitation. In the second stanza the dashes are more limited and controlled and the lines longer, more drawn out, allowing a dreamier, perhaps a wistful effect as she thinks of 'the Girl's life' which now looks so odd 'Behind this soft Eclipse'. The 'Eclipse' which is **metaphorically** marriage may be described positively as 'soft', but eclipses block something out, and the word can also suggest a loss of importance or power, especially through overshadowing by another. Here, does the husband now overshadow the wife? Then, in the first two lines of the last stanza a sense of hesitation returns. Is she trying to convince herself, perhaps, that if this, being wife, is comfort, the other, being girl, *must* have been pain? It is possible to see a hint of buried regret here which is further emphasised by the manner in which she finally prefers not to continue making any comparisons between the life of girl and wife. The tone becomes firmer, more assertive, even dismissive, and the dashes disappear to be replaced by the insistent exclamation marks: 'I'm "Wife"! Stop there!' A sense of firmness and **closure** is further suggested by the sudden change from **slant rhyme** in stanzas one and two to **exact rhyme** in this final stanza, as though the 'Wife' is putting an end to any further comparisons.

It is also possible that the speaker, the 'wife' in this poem, is treated with some mild **irony** by the poet. The poem is, in a way, a form of **dramatic monologue**. The speaker does not question why she should now have status; she simply accepts with some complacency that being a wife brings more social status. Dickinson's lyrics do not reveal a consistent position on marriage (see Themes, on Love & Marriage).

Czar until 1917, the emperor of Russia; more generally someone in authority
Eclipse the total or partial obscuring of one celestial body by another; it can also imply the loss of importance or power, especially through overshadowing by another

211 COME SLOWLY – EDEN! C.1860 (1890)

Desire and consummation

The speaker asks her 'Eden' to come slowly since those unused to such pleasures may be lost, like a bee lost in the balms of a flower.

'Come slowly – Eden!' As with so many Dickinson poems, our initial response is probably simply to be struck by the brilliance of her first line. But who or what does Eden represent in this poem; is it a person or a situation or, potentially, either and both? This desired person/situation is equated with earthly paradise, not the paradise that might be attained after death. For Dickinson, Eden is usually synonymous with sensuous pleasure. Consequently, it is appropriate that this Eden is also associated by the speaker with flowers; Eden possesses 'Jessamines' and 'Balms'. The speaker herself is reduced to a pair of lips, sipping at Eden. The poem then moves onto an even more figurative level with the speaker comparing the possible consummation of her desire with the consummation of a bee's desire when he enters the flower. He becomes 'lost in Balms', lost in the ecstasy he finds within.

Is the consummation of desire – something that happens **imagistically** with the bee but not literally with the speaker since she is left only sipping – projected as positive or negative through the bee simile? In some ways it must be positive: the bee is 'fainting', it has reached the flower late and needs what the flower offers. Furthermore, to be 'lost in Balms' is positive if we focus on the word 'Balms', something comforting and soothing. However, we are still left with the fact that the bee is 'lost'. Is the poem then suggesting the preferability of remaining just sipping? It would probably be wrong to read this as a cautionary poem about the dangers of giving in to the lover as the language is far too sensual and playful for this. While the warning about the possibility of being 'lost' is there, the emphasis is surely on the slow teasing the speaker prefers, deferring the fulfilment of desire, savouring slowly – sipping at – the delights that are offered. What happens when desire is fulfilled is more the subject of 'Did the Harebell loose her girdle' (213) to which you may wish to compare this poem. Perhaps what the speaker fears about the seductiveness of these balms is that she may become too absorbed in the other, 'lost' in the sense of losing the self. This is certainly what seems to have disturbed Dickinson most about marriage: the idea of subordinating the self to another (see Themes, on Love & Marriage).

How would the voice in this poem be described? Dickinson's **persona** in her love poetry is often rather coy and girlish, and this is suggested here by the 'Bashful' nature of the way the lips sip; they are 'unused to Thee', suggestive of innocence, virginity. The tone nevertheless also seems luxuriant, sensual; how is this achieved? The use of **enjambment** between the two stanzas certainly contributes, creating a long sweeping effect which is nevertheless kept to a slow and luxuriant pace by the use of the dashes. There is also the long **assonantal** 'e' sound which dominates the **rhyme** of the first stanza. What do you think of the change from passive to active in the speaker? The simile of the bee suggests that the speaker is like that bee, and that her Eden is like his flower. However, Eden, that which is desired, is in the first stanza the agent; it is active, advancing towards the receptive passive speaker. But as we move to the bee image, that which is desired, the flower, is placed in the passive position while the bee – standing in for the speaker – has become the active agent. This change in the speaker from passive to active, however, is perhaps begun in the first stanza as the lips begin sipping the nectar of Eden. The image of the bee entering the flower is, of course, undeniably sexual, and so there is some playing with gender roles here too: the bee is the male to the female flower, but the speaker, who is equated with the bee, seems feminised, the bashful passive one. Dickinson frequently, in her more sensual poems, places herself – or at least her speaker – in the position of the male: here she likens herself to the bee doing the entering rather than the flower being entered; similarly in 'Wild Nights – Wild Nights!' (249) she expresses the desire to 'moor – Tonight – / In Thee!' For this and other reasons her love poems have sometimes been read as homoerotic. Some critics, however, would say that gender is genuinely irrelevant in such poems as these: the poet is simply assuming a persona in much the same way as she assumes a masculine persona in 'A narrow Fellow in the Grass' (986). Others, however, suggest that Dickinson has a tendency to associate active sexuality with the masculine and passive with the feminine throughout. This seems quite a reasonable explanation, particularly since we are dealing with a nineteenth-century woman. Which explanation would you find most convincing?

Jessamines jasmine, which has intensely fragrant flowers
Balms something comforting and soothing; more particularly, *Melissa*, a pungent lemon-scented herb; also scented unguents from the resins used in healing

213 DID THE HAREBELL LOOSE HER GIRDLE   1860 (1891)

Once we possess what we desire, do we still value it as before?

When the bee takes possession of the harebell, does it still value or '*hallow*' the flower it so desired? Once we attain our Paradise, does it still seem to be an Eden?

This brief **lyric** works on three levels: first there is the literal description of the bee entering the harebell. On the second level, suggested by such things as the use of the word 'lover' to describe the bee, the poem applies the question to the relationship between lovers: will the lady who has been persuaded to yield be respected as much as before by her lover? On the third level, to which we are led by the other questions in stanza two, the lyric more generally asks if we inevitably value what we desire and cannot have and then devalue it once the object of desire has been attained.

Dickinson draws upon many different **personas** and voices in her poems about love and marriage; these include the playful and flirtatious, the passionate and sensual, the reverential and solemn, the quiet and submissive, and the **ironic** and sceptical. What kind of a persona is Dickinson constructing here and how would you describe the tone of voice? The use of **imagery** from the natural world, the flowers and the bees, suggests quite a childlike playfulness. This is emphasised by the simple lilting rhythm, and the repetition of word and sound which produce an almost nursery rhyme effect. You might find it useful to compare the resulting voice with the more sensual voice of another poem about a bee and flower, 'Come slowly – Eden!' (211).

214 **I** TASTE A LIQUOR NEVER BREWED – 1860 (1861)

An ecstatic description of being drunk on the joys of life

The speaker describes the 'liquor' in which she is indulging and which she will continue to imbibe even after death.

The central **metaphor** in this poem is that of intoxication, and yet the speaker is drunk on a 'liquor never brewed', a liquor far superior to that found in 'the Vats upon the Rhine'. Dickinson uses the idea of drunkenness to suggest a certain state of mind. How would you describe this state of mind? She is 'Inebriate of Air' and 'Debauchee of Dew'. It seems to be an ecstatic sense of delight she is describing; she is celebrating the sensual world, overcome by the beauty of the natural world around her. The tone is joyous, even boastful. She will drink, she claims, when all else is forced to stop. She will continue staggering from inn to inn. The mental feeling of intoxication is repeatedly described in concrete terms, drawing upon the **images** of literal, physical drunkenness. The concept of time enters in stanza three, with the idea of butterflies and bees being subject to seasonal changes; their pleasures will end when autumn arrives. She, however, will drink on into eternity, until, as the final stanza notes, heavenly beings rush to see her, 'the little Tippler / Leaning against the – Sun –'. This poem is full of word play, numerous words refer to an over-indulgence in alcohol, even though what the speaker indulges in is as harmless as 'Air' and 'Dew'.

The **metre** used here, as in so many Dickinson poems, is the **common** or ballad metre taken from hymnology. Compare the metre of this poem with, for example, the well-known hymn 'O God our help in ages past' (see Style, on Rhythm & Metre). How does Dickinson manage to create such a different – such an appropriately rollicking effect – while using the same basic metre as this solemn hymn? This seems to have something to do with her introduction of irregularities, as in the sudden movement caused by beginning on a stressed syllable in stanza two: 'Reeling – thro endless summer days –'. It is also the effect of her dashes and pauses and her joyful and assertive exclamations: 'I shall but drink the more!' There is also her choice of language and rhymes. The frequent **alliterative** and **assonantal** effects, for example, seem to move the poem along at a swinging pace, particularly in such lines as 'Inebriate of Air – am I – / And Debauchee of Dew –' and 'Till Seraphs swing their snowy Hats – / And Saints – to windows run –'. The comic disrespect with which she treats these heavenly beings – they are a great deal more active and human than one would normally expect – adds to the humorous and elated effect of the poem: everything here, even saints and seraphs, exudes energy.

The final image of the 'little Tippler / Leaning against the – Sun –' is reminiscent of a drunk leaning against a lamppost, but is there perhaps a more serious element introduced here? The 'Sun' is often used as an image for Christ (the 'son of God'), and the speaker is going to drink 'Till Seraphs swing their snowy Hats – / And Saints – to windows run –'. Is she going to drink, then, to indulge in and celebrate the beauty of the sensual world until she dies and goes to heaven, and is united with Christ, and perhaps continue even then? Dickinson's view of Christ and heaven certainly does not seem to be the traditional Puritan version (see Background). Furthermore, the emphasis is by no means on the afterlife but on the present life, on the material world and not the spiritual. Dickinson's treatment of nature here as in many other of her poems demonstrates how she differed in her approach to the natural world from the **Transcendentalists**. While such poets as Emerson sought to express the spirit of the world, to rise above the material to celebrate what lies beyond, it is the material world itself in which the speaker rejoices here. To transcend nature is not her aim; her aim is to celebrate the sensual world which she sees as providing a paradise equal to that offered by religion.

216 S AFE IN THEIR ALABASTER CHAMBERS –   1859 (1862), 1861 (1890)

Death and immortality

There are two versions of this **lyric**. Stanza one is virtually the same in each version. The dead lie in their graves, finally 'safe' from the world, awaiting resurrection. This **image** of the dead is juxtaposed in the first version of stanza two with images of a joyful natural world, and in the second version with images of a cold and indifferent universe.

1859 version: It is difficult to decide whether a positive image of the dead is actually presented in the first stanza, and whether this stanza does in fact suggest a confident faith – or even a desire for such faith – in resurrection and immortality. Is it important that the dead here lie in satin-lined coffins? In traditional Puritan belief, wealth was a sign of God's elect; this does not, of course, necessarily mean that the poem itself supports the apparent quiet assurance of the 'meek' dead awaiting resurrection. The first word of the poem, 'Safe', might give a certain smug confidence to the 'elect' that the poem suggests may not be justified. This unjustified smugness may also be implied by the manner in which the soft but heavy **alliterative** 'm' of 'meek members' is offset by the harder alliterative 'r' of 'Rafter' and 'Roof'. They may have their satin-lined coffins and their confidence in resurrection, but their reality is suggested by the way they are cut off from all vitality and sensation by the 'Roof of Stone'. The dead, in their 'Alabaster Chambers', one of Dickinson's most effective and chilling images, seem suspended in some cold white prison. They are untouched by 'Morning', associated with hope, or by 'Noon', which we might associate with fulfilment and intensity. All that is left for them is the unmentioned evening, or night, which suggests death. Repetition seems to function in this stanza to suggest a sense of timelessness and suspension, and this effect is emphasised by the slowness imposed upon the stanza by the **end stopped** lines. Stanza two contrasts the coldness and suspension of the dead with the vibrancy and activity of nature. The alliterative effects now change to support this sense of vibrancy as is demonstrated in such phrases as 'Light laughs the breeze' and 'Babbles the Bee'. Is Dickinson, with these natural images, offering consolation, the idea that in spite of the death of the individual, life continues, the cycle goes on? Alternatively, or in addition, is she using these natural images to emphasise the terrifying deprivation of vitality imposed by death?

1861 version: Do the small changes made in the second version of stanza one have any particular effect on your reading? In particular, consider how Dickinson makes the dash functional in the second version and how this dash, combined with the use of the exclamation mark, might subtly alter the **tone** and consequently also our interpretation. One of the effects is to throw the emphasis more upon that final phrase. The second stanza in this version, rather than contrasting the dead with the natural world, contrasts the dead with larger, even cosmic events. The slow movement of the planets and constellations continues, and in the face of this cosmic power, earthly power and material values seem unimportant. Those events which may appear to have great significance on earth, the rise and fall of political figures, for example, make no impression in the greater order of things. Again, alliterative effects make a significant contribution to the tone. 'Diadems – drop – and Doges – surrender – / Soundless as dots – on a Disc of Snow –'. Events on earth appear insignificant. Does the hard repetition of the 'd' sound add to a dismissive effect, or does it create an effect of bleakness, deadness, or perhaps both? The final line returns to the chilling visual image of whiteness introduced in the 'Alabaster Chambers' of the first line, but compounds the effect with the aural image of dots dropping soundlessly on a snowflake. The poem leaves us, then, with a sense of utter coldness and silence. How does this differ from the attitude towards the world with which we are left in the first version?

Some critics argue that Dickinson's apparent inability to choose between the two versions of this poem suggests the conflict she experienced between the desire for secure religious faith, hinted at in the first version, and a belief in cosmic indifference, offered by the second. Do you agree with this distinction between the two versions or do you think, as has been suggested here, that the attitude towards religious faith can be seen as ultimately quite similar in both?

Alabaster hard semi-transparent stone, known for its properties of smoothness and whiteness

Members of the Resurrection members of a group who believe in the resurrection of the individual after death. According to the Bible, Christ rose from the dead three days after his death; this was regarded as a sign that there was the possibility of a final resurrection for all men

Diadems crowns containing precious stones

Doges title of the chief magistrate in the republics of Venice (until 1797) and Genoa (until 1805)

254 'HOPE' IS THE THING WITH FEATHERS − 1861 (1891)

A celebration of the strength of hope

Hope is like a bird that perches in the soul. It never stops singing and never asks for anything in return for its song.

This is one of Dickinson's most straightforward poems of definition (see Themes, on Poems of Definition) in which an abstract mental state is presented in concrete terms. It also contains what is, for Dickinson, a relatively straightforward **metaphor**. The *tenor* here is 'Hope', the subject of the comparison, while 'the thing with feathers' (by implication a bird) is the *vehicle*, the metaphoric too. However, since it is so clear that she is comparing hope to a bird, why does she not say so directly; why instead say that it 'is the thing with feathers'? Feathers may emphasise certain qualities of the bird that, in the poem's focus upon the song, are not mentioned; specifically, this would refer to its ability to fly, to leave the mundane earth behind and revel in the freedom of the skies. Hope, similarly, is what gives us the ability to transcend the problems of the world. Furthermore, feathers suggest something soft and comforting, and somehow we do not expect Dickinson's bird to be a hawk.

Hawks, at any rate, tend not to perch and sing as this bird does. It perches in the soul and sings 'the tune without the words'. This seems relatively straightforward – birds after all having no words to sing – but in view of the fact that this is about hope, it is slightly more complicated. Dickinson seems to suggest that hope is the tune without words because hope is not limited to any one particular situation, and language – words – would limit it, perhaps, by explaining what the hope is about, the problems that led to the need for the comfort of hope. What Dickinson is interested in is the abstract, general principle. Do birds in fact keep singing through gales and storms? It is certainly true that a rain shower can start them all singing, but they do tend to disappear in storms. Here, she slightly distorts the bird's behaviour in order to emphasise the idea that hope seems to grow even stronger in difficult times. What is meant by those final lines 'never, in Extremity / It asked a crumb – of Me'? Hope helps us, but it does not require that we do anything for it to ensure its presence.

Metrically, this is an extremely regular poem, the only variation being in the first line, which begins with the stressed syllable 'Hope'. Dickinson is also quite sparing with her dashes here, and there are only a few pauses to interrupt the flow of the rhythm. The use of **anaphora**, in the lines beginning with 'And' and 'That', along with the **alliterative** 's', contribute to a sense of balance and harmony by providing links between stanzas. The result, appropriately enough considering the subject, is an intensely musical poem. Compare the language and images used here with those of two other poems about hope: 'Hope is a strange invention –' (1392) and 'Hope is a subtle Glutton –' (1547).

258 THERE'S A CERTAIN SLANT OF LIGHT 1861 (1890)

A description of winter light and its effects

Oppressive winter light generates a transformation in the observer. The poem moves from a description of the external landscape to the inner landscape and then conflates the two in the final stanza.

The poem begins with an attempt to capture the essence of a certain kind of winter light. Light is associated with brightness and clarity, but this kind of thin winter light that is being described is oppressive, alienating; it is, **paradoxically**, a light which darkens the soul. The second stanza moves us from an external to an internal landscape in order to consider further the effects of this light upon us. 'Heavenly Hurt' it gives us: this is some kind of religious experience and it alters us radically. Where it alters us, however, is unclear: 'internal difference' is experienced 'Where the Meanings, are –'. While it is tempting to identify the feeling induced by this winter light simply as despair, such a neat and orderly summing up is not actually endorsed. Dickinson suggests that the exact nature of this feeling is elusive: 'None may teach it' to anyone. It is awe-inspiring and afflictive, a moment of spiritual revelation brought on by the natural phenomenon of winter light. It provokes despair, but is not, in itself, despair. This is one of many Dickinson poems in which the cause remains uncertain and the focus is placed instead on capturing the nature of the effects. The final stanza merges internal and external landscapes as the breathless awe of the speaker is projected onto a **personified** landscape and more boundaries are undercut as the division between human and nature dissolves.

In attempting to convey the feeling induced by this kind of winter light, the first stanza employs a **simile** which involves **synaesthesia**. Winter light, a visual image, is described as being 'like the Heft / Of Cathedral Tunes'. Instead of associating winter light with the light that might filter through the stained-glass windows of a cathedral, Dickinson associates it with the sound of cathedral music; this aural image is further complicated by that word 'Heft', which indicates weight, and offers a tactile image. The light is oppressive physically as well as mentally. Synaesthesia frequently functions, as it does here, to break down normal categories, to undermine boundaries between the senses. The synaesthetic associations, then, help to contribute to a sense of unease and disturbance. The effects of the light combine the concrete and the abstract: it is oppressive spiritually, but its weight is also felt physically. What techniques does Dickinson use to convey this feeling of oppression to the reader? She consistently uses **exact rhymes**, for example; can they be said to contribute in any way to a sense of gloom and heaviness? The word choice is also important. Dickinson's first editors actually changed 'Heft' to 'weight'. What do you think would be lost if we had retained their version? Why is 'Heft' so much more appropriate and functional?

This light, however, is not only oppressive; it is also impressive, awe-inspiring. How is this conveyed through the language? What is suggested by, for example, the description of the affliction as an 'imperial affliction'? A sense of awe is also suggested in the final stanza through Dickinson's use of **pathetic fallacy**. The external landscape has affected the inner landscape of the speaker and now, in this last stanza, the speaker's feelings are projected back upon the external world. The speaker's emotions are enacted by the landscape and the shadows. Do you think the use of the dashes in this final stanza is functional, and would anything be lost if they were removed? Do the significant pauses which the dashes impose perhaps further emphasise a sense of breathless waiting?

Seal a word full of resonance in this context. It is a device impressed upon a piece of wax, fixed to a document as a mark of authentication; it can mean to close up or secure; it is also a term found in Revelation, for example, 5.1 'a book ... sealed with seven seals'; in Calvinism, sacraments are seals of the covenant by which God affirms his promise of salvation to the elect; here all that is promised is despair

280 I FELT A FUNERAL, IN MY BRAIN   1861 (1896)

A description of a mental experience

Imagistically drawing upon the progression of a funeral, the **lyric** traces the stages of some kind of mental breakdown.

The lyric begins by establishing the basic proposition of the poem: the speaker has had some kind of mental experience which is likened to the events of a funeral: a psychological death becomes merged with a physical death. In the speaker's mind, the mourners seem to be walking up and down, perhaps paying their last respects to the dead person lying in the coffin. They are then seated and the funeral service begins. Once this stage of the ritual is complete, the coffin is lifted and taken to the graveyard while the church bell tolls. The coffin is placed on planks set over the grave and then one of the planks breaks and the coffin drops down into the grave, suggesting perhaps the mind's final plunge into the abyss of despair.

We are never told what produces the particular effects upon the speaker described in this lyric. Although the use of the funeral as the central image might suggest something has died within her, the focus here is upon the description of the emotional experience itself, upon the effects and not their cause, the cause which, as in so many Dickinson poems, remains unclear. The funeral imagery, mourners, coffin, service and bell serve to give concrete form to abstract feelings. How does Dickinson create a sense of mounting pressure and tension in the first two stanzas? To start with, the repetition of 'treading' and 'beating' suggests a relentless force acting upon the mind, something rhythmic and repetitious and numbing. This poem is full of instances in which Dickinson depends on sounds that suggest their meaning: the constant **alliterative** 'b' is the major example ('Brain', 'beating', 'Box', boots, 'Bell', 'Being', 'broke'), suggestive of a repetitive thump that becomes unbearable. An oppressive atmosphere is immediately created with the description of feet pounding up and down, creating an almost unbearable repetitive sound, a sound which is then emphasised by the **simile** which compares the service to a beating drum.

The sense which is emphasised throughout this lyric is that of hearing: all the events in the funeral are suggested through increasingly intense sounds, treading, beating, creaking, repetitive sounds that build up until we reach the **synaesthetic** description of space itself appearing 'to toll'. At this point it appears as though there is nothing in the world but a tolling bell, and the speaker herself is reduced to an ear, isolated from everything and everyone but that deafening bell which fills her mind with one shattering tone. The final separation of the speaker from the world comes with the breaking of the plank and the loss of reason; there is now nothing left to support her, no rational thought at all. The whole poem moves towards this moment of falling into an abyss, and even the rhyme scheme can be said to emphasise this movement. The first four stanzas use **exact rhyme** for lines two and four ('fro' and 'through' probably being exact rhyme in nineteenth-century New England dialect). In the final stanza, however, as reason breaks down and the mind plunges into despair, the established rhyme pattern simultaneously breaks down with the sudden use of **slant rhyme** in 'down' and 'then'.

We are told that the speaker 'Finished knowing – then –'. It has been suggested this means that after breaking through the bounds of reason the speaker finishes by knowing something; if so, what becomes known remains unclear to us; we are simply left with the dash. Alternately, we could simply see the line as suggesting the complete loss of *all* thought, understanding, knowledge. Taking the poem as a whole into account, which reading do you find most convincing? Is it possible to accept both, even though they may appear contradictory? Although frequently interpreted as the tracing of a descent into despair, this lyric has also been read as a descent into madness, as representing an actual funeral through the mind of the dead person, and, more convincingly, as a description of the loss of consciousness. Can you find textual evidence in support of these alternate readings?

303 THE SOUL SELECTS HER OWN SOCIETY –   1862 (1890)

The self-sufficiency of the soul

The soul is undisturbed by the external world, noting, but remaining unmoved by, the signs of activity and the temptations outside her door.

The speaker describes the soul as though it were a woman in her home, content and secure. She selects her own society and shuts the door on the 'divine Majority' who wish her to become part of their society. She notices but is unmoved by the chariots which pause at her gate, ceremonial carriages which suggest she is being offered power and position, and by the emperor who kneels on her mat. After this description the speaker notes that she has known the soul, confronted by many, to 'Choose One' and then pay no further attention to anyone else.

> There are two main levels of language and **imagery** in this poem. There is the domestic language and the homely images of a woman within her home, content to shut the door on the outside world, while carriages pause at her gate and emperors kneel on her doormat. There is also the religious language and imagery of selection or election which could be drawn from Dickinson's Puritan background (see Historical & Literary Background). One of the doctrines of Calvin was that God chooses certain individuals for salvation without reference to their faith or works. Furthermore, Puritans elected those who were considered worthy and without sin to be members of the church and the minister of the church would be elected by a majority vote. Here the soul is responsible for election; she elects her own society, and chooses to reject the society of the 'divine Majority'.

> Conventional notions about power are reversed in this **lyric**. To have power here does not involve the glory offered by religion, or the glory possessed by those in control in the outside world, those who rule over others. Instead, it is the ability to construct a world for oneself. Could there be some **ambiguity** about the first line however; that is, does the soul select a specific person or persons for her society, someone else, or does the soul decide to remain content with her own society, does she choose complete isolation? The poem has been read both ways, although the former reading fits in more easily with the way the soul chooses 'One', the one perfect companion, in the final stanza.

> Do you think that varying line lengths and the alternation between **feminine** and **masculine rhymes** in this poem serve any function? The feminine rhymes fall at the end of the first and third lines in each stanza, lines which are, at least in the second and third stanzas, noticeably longer than the second and fourth lines. Does the combination of these techniques, perhaps, offer a formal contrast between amplitude and limitation? By the time we reach the last

stanza the second and fourth lines, with their rather hard **slant masculine rhymes**, have become very abrupt, final, containing only two syllables, and they reflect a sense of closing off which appropriately enacts the moment when the soul has chosen 'One' and then decides to 'close the Valves of her attention – / Like Stone'. How do you respond to the use of the word 'Valves' in this mixed **metaphor**? The archaic meaning of valves as the parts of a folding door reinforces the domestic image of the first stanza when the soul shuts the door of her house. If the word is read anatomically, however, it may make us think of the valve, and the closing off, of the heart, perhaps closing off the flow, then, of the emotions. The use of the word 'Stone', something impenetrable and unfeeling, emphasises this hardening, suggesting walls, perhaps, that separate the soul from the outside world. In this sense, can the isolation described be a form of confinement as well as a form of contentment?

divine Majority spiritual electors: an assembly which elects members of its society

Chariots light, four-wheeled horse-drawn ceremonial carriage

Valves a valve is any device that starts, shuts off and regulates the flow of a fluid. Anatomically, it refer to a flaplike structure in an organ, like the heart, that controls the passage of fluid through that organ. The archaic meaning of valves is the leaves or two halves of a folding door

315 H E FUMBLES AT YOUR SOUL   1862 (1896)

A description of someone or something acting upon the soul

Someone acts upon the soul like a player at the piano, preparing the soul for the final climactic moment of full assault. An **image** is drawn from the natural world to provide some kind of comment upon this human experience.

This poem is primarily based upon a musical **analogy**: someone – an unspecified He – acts upon 'your Soul / As Players at the Keys'. The Soul appears like an instrument, perhaps a piano, which this 'He' is playing, first fumbling at the keys, as though warming up. This is a preparatory activity: the soul is being prepared for the moment when

'He' will 'drop full Music on'. The music gradually gains in intensity, but this happens so slowly that the one being acted upon has time to get used to the sounds. Then, just as the Soul begins to relax, to feel calm again, there is the climactic moment of assault: 'One – imperial – Thunderbolt' which 'scalps your naked Soul'. This is one of many Dickinson poems where confidently assigning a referent to a 'He' – or to an 'It' is difficult, and the nature of the participants is left open in order to focus specially upon the nature of the experience.

What kind of experience is this? We can say that we have an active 'He' working upon a passive 'you', but can we say if this experience is ultimately a positive and creative one, or a negative and invasive one? The musical analogy on which this poem is based might suggest a creative process. Something will be produced out of this interaction between player and instrument; the gradual preparation is leading up to the moment when he drops 'full Music on'. This analogy, however, still leaves us unclear about what he will do to the Soul that is the equivalent of dropping full music on. While 'Keys' suggests a piano, it also suggests someone trying to gain entrance with the keys to a lock, and in this sense the poem might indicate invasion as well as creativity. The images certainly become increasingly violent; words like 'stuns' and 'Blow' and 'Hammers' suggest aggression. Now there seems to be some respite, perhaps the 'you' gradually becoming accustomed to the invasion: 'Your Breath has time to straighten – / Your Brain – to bubble Cool –'. The brain seems to have been heated to such a degree that it is about to boil over. Then, just at this moment He 'Deals – One – imperial – Thunderbolt – / That scalps your naked Soul –'. Compare the effect of the word 'scalps', with its sense of decisive violence and aggression, with the original 'fumbles'. Also consider the fact that at this point the soul is now described as 'naked'. How has the soul been reduced to this state, left so helpless and exposed, and how has the relationship between the 'He' and the 'you' changed? Although most of the language discussed so far is violent and aggressive, there is nevertheless an indication that there is something positive about this experience. The 'Blow' that the soul is being prepared to receive is an 'Ethereal' one, and the Thunderbolt which ultimately scalps the Soul is 'imperial'. What is suggested by the use of such words? The climax, as Cristanne Miller has observed, 'is as ecstatic as it is devastating; the tension of the poem resides in its perfect commingling of the sensations of breathless anticipation and terror' (*Emily Dickinson: A Poet's Grammar*).

Dickinson makes particularly effective use of the dash in this poem. In the lines 'By fainter Hammers – further heard – / Then nearer – Then so slow', for example, the dashes impose pauses which suggest gradual closing in and intensifying of the sound. Similarly, in 'Deals – One – imperial – Thunderbolt – / That scalps your naked Soul' the dashes in the first line initially slow down the movement of the poem to place intense emphasis upon each single word; the action is deliberate and sure, and builds up slowly until the dashes suddenly disappear in the second line to sweep us away into that horrific but ecstatic final moment.

It is not clear how the final lines relate to the rest of the poem. They are offset from the previous lines, are unrhymed, have the nature of an **aphorism**, and suggest both separation and connection. Should we assume that the winds taking 'the Forests in their Paws' are similar to the scalping of the Soul, or is this offered as a contrast? Are these final lines intended to explain or throw new light on the events previously described? Dickinson does not tell us the answer. The winds seem aggressive since they are described like wild beasts, but on the other hand their aggression is combined with gentleness: they take the Forests in their 'Paws', not their 'claws'. 'Paws', of course, also includes some word play on 'pause'. The universe is still, everything pauses in anticipation, and the dashes help convey this sense of breathless waiting. The rhythm has been smoothed out, regularised, and consequently suggests a more peaceful moment. We are left not knowing the result of this encounter. The final dash, eliminating any sense of closure, simply suggests that something is about to happen, something so momentous that the whole universe becomes 'still'.

The identity of the unspecified 'He' in this poem has been the focus of much critical analysis. It has variously been suggested that 'He' may be God, death, a lover, or poetry itself. Early **biographical** interpretations read this as the description of a romantic relationship, and many pages were devoted to assessing the most likely candidate to be Dickinson's lover. Alternately, it was thought that 'He' was a preacher and Dickinson was describing his effects upon a congregation. The poem has also been read as an expression of the poet's fear of the masculine. More recently, **feminist** readings have suggested that the subject of the poem is gender relationships. The active force is clearly specified as a 'He', but the gender of the 'you' remains unspecified. A surprising number of critics nevertheless assume the passive object of his actions is a 'she'; do you think this is a reasonable assumption to make? It probably would not be reasonable to make such an assumption purely on the basis that Dickinson is a female poet. She does not necessarily always have to be focusing upon female experiences. However, since Dickinson (and her twentieth-century readers) lived in a culture which associated the masculine with the active subject and the feminine with the passive object, perhaps the assumption is justifiable. Furthermore, it is true that Dickinson often matches a female victim with a threatening and authoritarian male figure in her poetry. If we do accept the actors in the poem can be defined as a 'he' and a 'she', then perhaps the poem can be read as being about the power structures in male-female relationships.

322 THERE CAME A DAY AT SUMMER'S FULL 1861 (1890)

The ecstasy of a lovers' brief meeting

The speaker describes a day of joy when she was briefly united with her lover. The time passes quickly, and they part, believing that after years of suffering and separation they will be reunited in heaven.

This poem has sometimes been read as though Dickinson were describing the apocalyptic marriage with the Lamb that is described in Revelation; that would make this a poem of Christian consolation: the speaker saying that although she cannot be united with her earthly lover, she will ultimately be a bride of Christ. Most critics now, however, would argue that Dickinson is only appropriating religious language and doctrine in order to define the speaker's relationship with an earthly lover: Christian and specifically Calvinist doctrine and language are used to construct her own theology of secular love (see Historical & Literary Background, on The Puritan Heritage).

In stanza one, the speaker recalls a day on which she was briefly united with her lover: 'There came a Day at Summer's full'. Literally this refers to the summer solstice, 21 June, the longest day in the summer. To describe this as 'Summer's full', however, effectively suggests a sense of fulfilment and completion. The ecstasy of the meeting with the lover is so overwhelming that she thought this feeling could be experienced only by saints once they reached heaven. Stanza two describes the apparent ordinariness of the day: the sun and the flowers are oblivious to the special nature of the occasion. Time passes as usual: the sun measures out the course of the day; the flowers 'blew', perhaps suggesting that they continue to lose their petals. Nothing stands still.

In stanza three, the focus moves to the meeting of the lovers. 'The time was scarce profaned, by speech'. There is no need for them to speak, and the religious suggestiveness of 'profaned' prepares us for the **analogy** that follows. Words are 'needless, as at Sacrament, / The Wardrobe – of our Lord –'. Calvinist doctrine limited the sacraments to baptism and the Lord's Supper – marriage is not a Calvinist sacrament. The Calvinist sacrament of the Lord's Supper rejected the Catholic notion of transubstantiation, and emphasised the spiritual nourishment provided by the physical symbols of bread and wine. The two sacraments of baptism and the Lord's Supper were seen as seals of the Covenant of Grace appointed by God to be signs, pledges of his mercy to humankind through the crucified Christ; they were the means by which God affirmed his promise of salvation to the elect. What the lovers have is a new sacrament, analogous to the Sacrament of the Lord's supper in that it too promises something after death – reunion with the lover, however, a different kind of grace.

Stanza four begins with another religious analogy: 'Each was to each The Sealed Church'. This may be a scriptural reference, drawing upon the idea of the Lamb's book in Revelation, the sealed book which is broken open to reveal the future. In the secular context in which the phrase is used, Dickinson could be looking forward not to final judgement but to the fulfilment of love in heaven. It might also be a sacramental reference. In Calvinist doctrine, the phrase represented all the elect included in the Covenant of Grace which was sealed, that is, confirmed, promised, by the two sacraments of baptism and the Lord's Supper. Here, there are only two elect, the speaker and her lover; each is Christ to the other, and they have a new kind of sacrament. They are allowed to partake, to 'commune': 'Lest we too awkward show / At Supper of the Lamb'. This might initially suggest their communion is a preparation, a rehearsal for the Supper of the Lamb, the wedding banquet in the New Jerusalem, the union with Christ (Revelation 19). But if each is Christ to each, then it is again clear that what they anticipate is their own reunion.

In stanza five, there is a return to images of time passing, as in stanza two; now, however, time seems to be slipping away even more quickly. The opening scene of sun and flowers is replaced by an **analogy** of 'faces on two Decks' that look back at each other while 'Bound to opposing lands'. A sense of gradual fragmentation, falling apart, is suggested by the use of the hands and the faces, the parts rather than the whole, in this stanza. The moment of separation is approaching fast. When all the 'time had leaked', in stanza six, 'Each bound the Other's Crucifix – / We gave no other Bond –'. The crucifix is suffering; they are crucified, separated, condemned to suffer. Their suffering in love is suggested in the final stanza by the phrase their 'Calvaries of Love', Calvary being the place where Christ was crucified. This suffering will justify their reunion after death, in a 'new Marriage'. There is little sense here that heaven itself will be of much importance; what is important is that it will allow for this final union between the lovers. The poem ends, therefore, on a hopeful note, and with the word 'Love'. You might want to compare this with the total absence of hope for the lovers, even after death, in 'I cannot live with You –' (640), where the final word, appropriately, is 'Despair'.

Where Resurrections – be – that is, in heaven
solstice either the shortest or the longest day of the year

Sacrament Christian rites of special significance generally seen as an outward and visible sign of an inward and spiritual grace. The Protestant sacraments are baptism and communion; the Roman Catholic sacraments further include such rites as penance, confirmation, and the Eucharist, in which the Last Supper is commemorated by the consecration of bread and wine – the body and blood of Christ. Calvinist doctrine saw the sacrament as a seal of the covenant by which God affirmed his promise of salvation to the elect, and limited the sacraments to baptism and the Lord's Supper.

Sealed Church this may be a scriptural reference, drawing upon the idea of the Lamb's book in Revelation, the sealed book which is broken open to reveal the future. In Calvinist doctrine, the phrase represented all the elect included in the Covenant of Grace sealed, that is, confirmed, promised, by the two sacraments of baptism and the Lord's Supper

Supper of the Lamb the wedding banquet of the Lamb, suggesting the union of the saved with Christ: 'Happy are those who are invited to the wedding banquet of the Lamb' (Revelation 19.9)

Calvaries Calvary is the place outside the walls of Jerusalem where Jesus was crucified; a calvary can refer to any representation of Christ's crucifixion and even, more generally, to any experience involving great suffering

328 A BIRD CAME DOWN THE WALK – 1862 (1891)

The speaker's observations of a bird

The speaker, unobserved, watches a bird come down the path, eat a worm and drink dew. She offers him a crumb and at that moment the bird flies away into the air.

The speaker describes to us with precise, clear, concrete detail what she sees the bird do. He bites a worm in half and eats it raw, the slight shock registered here by the speaker emphasising the destructive, primitive side of nature. The bird then drinks some dew from a grass and hops sideways, momentarily frightened by a beetle. It looks around and the suggestion of the bird's fear is intensified. The speaker tries to offer it a crumb and at that moment the bird takes off into the air, safe, serene, and beautiful.

For most of this poem the **tone** is conversational. This conversational tone is emphasised by the use of **anaphora**, and by the rhythms. The quick **trimeter** lines of the opening stanzas, varied by one **tetrameter**, suggest the quick movements of the bird as it hops around. The language is clear and simple, and the descriptions highly concrete. The pauses also add to a certain sprightliness that might be said to echo the movements of the bird itself. In the first stanza, for example, the dashes at the end of lines one and two create pauses which suggest the speaker, narrating her story, is making an aside to the reader. Similarly, the comma before 'raw' imposes another pause, emphasising the rhyme and suggesting a slight distaste or shock perhaps, at the manner in which the bird consumes his dinner. But with the third stanza something changes; the pattern established is disrupted. First, there is a change from **exact rhyme** to **slant rhyme** in the second and fourth lines. Furthermore, at the end of stanzas 1 and 2 there is a definite pause, the last line in each stanza is **end stopped** and so the stanzas can be seen as discrete closed units. But stanza three allows for no pause; the last line is **enjambed**: we are encouraged to keep reading without a pause into the next line, which happens to be the first line of the next stanza. What happens to the meaning as a result of this enjambed line? Who seems cautious and like 'one in danger': the bird or the speaker – or is the first in danger and the second cautious? It is **ambiguous** and Dickinson's compressed use of language, her enjambed line, allow us to interpret the moment both ways. Bird and speaker somehow become confused through the language, the distinctions between self and other or subject and object are weakened.

At this point, something else happens; as the bird takes off in flight, the language changes. That conversational, precise and concrete narrative flow is replaced by something quite luxuriantly poetic and abstract in the final stanza. Dickinson now uses such poetic techniques as **alliteration**, with the repeated 's' and 'b' sounds, the 'p' and 'l' sounds are blended, and long vowel sounds dominate the lines with the **assonance** of 'o' and 'a'. This change in the language is accompanied by a change in how the bird is viewed. The speaker's vision of the world alters and the bird itself is altered, becoming the focal point for this vision of a new world. Time and space shift; water, sky, and earth merge 'Too silver for a seam –'. The bird flies, swims, sails, leaps in this new element, and the speaker relies upon **images** which blend movement through water with movement through air. What are the Banks of Noon, and how can the abstract concept of time be turned into something so concrete, so physical, that we are provided with a visual picture of noon as a riverbank? What does rowing softer home mean, and how does this contribute towards capturing the way in which the bird flies? Dickinson might be trying to suggest alternative spheres of existence with which we are not familiar but of which the speaker has a momentary vision: the bird, in taking off, flying, provides her with an imaginative vision of an alternative reality, of what the world might seem like to that bird. She sees like the bird might – taking us back to that initial change when speaker and bird seem conflated. On the other hand, Dickinson might be emphasising the strangeness of the bird through her description, emphasising that it lives in a world totally alien to her. Which do you think is the most convincing reading?

plashless a less common word for splashless

341 AFTER GREAT PAIN, A FORMAL FEELING COMES – 1862 (1929)

A description of the numbing after-effects of pain

The poem analyses the condition of the mind following the experience of great pain. This mental experience is described using concrete language and **images** associated with the body, with nature, and with physical death. The opening line argues that the result of great pain is not hysteria or violent emotional distress but instead, rather surprisingly, a 'formal feeling', something associated with great control. There is no specific **persona** identified in this poem; the person described is instead identified only through parts of the body, the nerves, the heart, the feet, parts which are given an individual existence. There is a gradual movement towards a hardening, a numbness, paralysis, towards 'the Hour of Lead', a moment which is always remembered, even if eventually 'outlived'. The poem concludes with an **analogy** between the experience described and the experience of freezing to death.

How does Dickinson's use of individual parts of the body instead of a specific persona contribute towards the overall impression of numbness and rigidity that defines the poem? She is using the parts of the body **synecdochally** for the person, more particularly, the person's mind. The nerves, **personified**, sit 'ceremonious, like Tombs', a **simile** which suggests people sitting at a funeral service, and emphasises the idea of formality. The heart is 'stiff', which also suggests formality; it is questioning, but also controlled, perhaps trying to connect its suffering with that of Christ on the cross, but here the syntax is confused, suggesting confusion in the heart itself, the heart which can no longer even tell when the suffering began: 'Yesterday, or Centuries before?' The feet move in a 'mechanical' manner, and they 'go round', suggestive of aimlessness, in a 'Wooden way'; there is repetition of movement without meaning, without progress. The pauses which occur between so many of the words in this stanza emphasise this lack of progression. And yet Dickinson implies that there is a **paradoxical** serenity which can follow pain and suffering. There is a movement towards a 'Quartz contentment' – a description which fuses the concrete and the abstract, and which is qualified by the **simile** 'like a stone'. This contributes to the idea of loss of feeling – becoming numb as a stone – and yet paradoxically also indicates there is a feeling of contentment in this loss of feeling. The condition of the mind is finally brilliantly summarised and defined in the opening line of the last stanza: 'This is the Hour of Lead'. What is being combined in this highly compact **metaphor**? Time, something abstract, weighs down heavily upon the speaker: it becomes something tangible like lead, something unbearably dark, heavy, physical. There has been a gradual movement towards a hardening of everything and now there is nothing left but a sense of heavy numbness. The effect of great pain is, again rather paradoxically, the absence of all pain, the absence, indeed, of all feeling. This is basically the essence of the 'formal feeling'; it is a paradox: it is the feeling of no feeling. The highly compact metaphor found in 'This is the Hour of Lead' is now itself expanded upon in the last two lines with a simile which summarises the ideas of the poem; the process has been similar to that of freezing to death: 'First – Chill – then Stupor – then the letting go –'. The chill indicates the pain that has preceded the feeling described; the stupor is the emotional response to pain described in the poem; the letting go, which projects into the future, suggests what will hopefully happen next: the move from this 'formal feeling' to 'letting go' of it. This last line also offers a fine example of how effectively Dickinson could use the dash. The dashes here impose pauses, slow down our reading of the line so that as we read it the line almost seems to re-enact the slow process of freezing to death.

Quartz a colourless mineral

401 WHAT SOFT – CHERUBIC CREATURES – 1862 (1896)

A satiric attack on contemporary gentlewomen

The overrefined 'gentlewomen' are horrified by the imperfections of human nature and ashamed of the 'commonness' of Christianity.

Stanza one mocks the weak and soft natures of overrefined contemporary gentlewomen, comparing them to soft plush and bright but distant stars. Their convictions or beliefs are described in the second stanza as flimsy. These women are horrified by the imperfections of human nature; they are also ashamed of the Deity, of God who created human nature and assumed human form. The last stanza begins with two lines **parodying** the languid tones of these women, suggesting they would disdain the rough fishermen who became Christ's apostles, even disdain Christianity itself since the glory it can confer is available to all. The final two lines return to the voice of the original speaker and express the hope that, after this lady dies, Christ will ultimately be as ashamed of her.

How do we know that the adjectives 'Soft' and 'Cherubic', more normally seen as positive comments, are used in a derogatory manner in the opening line of this poem? The dashes could be said to contribute to this effect, and also the soft **assonance** and 's' **alliteration** which centres on 'Plush'. The language in this first stanza also effectively suggests the characters of these women. Their soft, yielding natures are effectively conveyed with the reference to 'Plush', something velvety but pliant, even spongy. Their aloofness, on the other hand, is suggested by the comparison with stars. Stars may be beautiful to look at, but they are very distant, even associated with coldness, an icy perfection. The use of the violent words 'assault' and 'violate' shocks in this context; the women seem too refined, too unemotional, to be associated with such aggressive words. Overall, how would you describe the **tone** in this first stanza: disdainful, contemptuous, perhaps? Why should the convictions of these gentlewomen be described as 'Dimity'? Dimity is a flimsy white fabric and the poem suggests the women's convictions are similarly flimsy. They are horrified by 'freckled' human nature, freckled suggesting human nature is, as it is, imperfect, flawed. At this point, it is useful to remember that the first line of the poem identifies the women as 'creatures', a word which emphasises that they too are part of human nature. But, as the last line here claims, these woman are also 'ashamed' of 'Deity'.

The final stanza provides the explanation of this rather surprising claim through an imitation of the voice of one of these ladies: 'It's such a common – Glory – / A Fisherman's – Degree'. How would you describe the tone of this woman? She sounds superior, disdainful: Christ came to earth in human form, he began a religion which is available to all and he chose simple fishermen as his disciples. When the speaker responds to the words of this imagined lady, a representative of her type, she hopes, using Redemption **metonymically** for Christ or God, that when the woman reaches heaven Christ will be equally ashamed of her. Why do you think Dickinson uses the word 'Brittle' to describe the gentlewoman? This can mean not only abrasive but also easily broken. Is the implication perhaps that Christ will 'break' them?

Plush   a fabric with a long and very soft pile, here used as in a plush chair
Dimity   a light cotton fabric

414 'TWAS LIKE A MAELSTROM, WITH A NOTCH   1862 (1945)

The speaker describes an experience concerning which she cannot decide whether it would have been better to perish or survive it

The experience described is first likened to being nearly sucked into a maelstrom or whirlpool and then released. Then the speaker compares the experience with being nearly destroyed by a Goblin until, just at the last moment, God saves her. Finally, she associates the feeling with the experience of being condemned to death and then, just at the last moment, granted a reprieve.

The speaker in this poem is attempting to describe some kind of psychic experience, but what 'it' is remains unclear. Critics have alternatively suggested the feeling to be caused by losing a lover, fear at the prospect of death and the onset of madness. Do you think the experience described should really be limited in such a way? Is there evidence for these interpretations or do you find them questionable and even reductive? As in many of Dickinson's so-called 'poems of definition', the attempt to define this abstract experience – whatever it may be – proceeds by comparing it to more easily definable, more physical and concrete experiences. The first two stanzas draw upon **images** from nature, offering the comparison of getting closer and closer to a maelstrom; a maelstrom is a large and powerful whirlpool which sucks into itself all objects within a certain radius, and so this comparison quite effectively suggests the awful fear and anticipation that such an experience would create. But what, we might ask, is a maelstrom 'with a notch'? The phrase itself, like the poem as a whole, is suggestive, but not explainable. The maelstrom gets closer and closer 'Until the Agony / Toyed coolly with the final inch / Of your delirious Hem –'. Here Dickinson draws upon **synecdoche**, with the hem of the dress standing for the person, and more particularly the person's mind. That hem is also **personified**, described as 'delirious'. The reactions of the victim here contrast strikingly with the qualities of the force by which she is being overtaken: it may be 'boiling', but it nevertheless toys 'coolly' with her.

The second two stanzas move from the natural world to a dramatic fictional situation, comparing the experience with being in the power of a goblin and saved just at the last moment. This goblin holds a 'Gauge' in his 'Paws', with which he measures the time left to the victim. Again, the victimiser seems coolly waiting, measuring, and in total control, while she is unable to move. Just at the last minute, a forgetful God remembers, and, almost as an aside, the dashes suggest, saves her. Finally, the last **analogy** focuses upon the last-minute reprieve of a convict about to be executed. How do we know that the dungeon described is not a tangible place but a psychic state? There is the sudden use of quite abstract vocabulary in 'Dungeon's luxury of Doubt'. This seems to suggest that if within the dungeon there is the luxury of doubt, then there is also the possibility of hope. Once she is 'frozen led' out of this dungeon, all hope disappears; it is as though she is already dead: the 'Film had stitched your eyes'. At this moment, an unspecified creature gasps 'Reprieve'. If the place in which all this anguish is taking place is actually a mental space, could this suggest that the aggressive other, here variously identified as Maelstrom and Goblin, is actually part of the self?

Maelstrom a large powerful whirlpool

501 THIS WORLD IS NOT CONCLUSION 1862 (1896)

An examination of the grounds on which faith in an afterlife is based

The poem begins with a confident assertion that there is an afterlife. Gradually, however, the assertion is qualified. Philosophy, sagacity, scholarship are not trustworthy sources of faith. Martyrs have suffered and died for the faith, but faith 'slips'. Faith clutches at twigs for support and is happy to go whichever way the wind is blowing. The church is theatrical and loud. Sermons and hymns may act like narcotics, stupefying one into apparent submission, but they cannot ease gnawing doubts, the 'tooth / That nibbles at the soul –'.

There is an **aphoristic** quality to the opening pronouncement in this poem, which conveys a sense of finality and conclusion: 'This World is not Conclusion. / A Species Stands beyond –'. This is one of the few poems in which Dickinson ends her first line with a full stop, in itself quite an indication of conclusiveness. There are also echoes of conventional religious pronouncements here in such ideas as heaven being 'Invisible'. However, even in these opening lines there is, perhaps, the seed of doubt. Why, after all, should Dickinson choose that word 'Species', with all its scientific associations, for the life which lies beyond? Darwin's *On the Origin of Species* had appeared in 1859, probably a few years before the poem was written. The tone changes with the idea that 'It beckons, and it baffles'. These two words, 'beckons' and 'baffles', suggest the idea of the afterlife pulling us in two ways: we are attracted, wanting to know, but we are nevertheless always disappointed, left simply confused. The **alliterative** 'b' creates a less ponderous, more informal and conversational air, and this is further emphasised by the following line 'Philosophy – don't know –', with its colloquial 'don't'. What do you think it means that 'through a Riddle, at the last – / Sagacity, must go –'? The 'Riddle' might be death itself, through which we must pass before we will be enlightened about whether the afterlife exists or not.

Faith itself is **personified**, presented as a young girl who slips, and that word 'slips' suggests both the abstract concept of loss of faith and the more concrete **image** of the physical movement of tripping. This visual image is further developed as 'Faith' 'laughs, and rallies' and 'Blushes' if anyone sees her tripping. She 'Plucks at a twig of Evidence', the impressiveness of her evidence undermined by the dismissive 'twig'. Why should it be ridiculous to ask a weather vane the way? A weather vane simply changes direction with the wind. Faith here seems somewhat helpless.

From the way in which the speaker describes church in the final lines, what would you say her attitude was towards formal religion? 'Much Gesture' suggests a touch of over-dramatisation, while the 'Strong Hallelujahs' that roll through the air imply a somewhat over-enthusiastic and perhaps automatic, unthinking response from the congregation. The final two lines, like the first, have an aphoristic quality. What is the effect of Dickinson describing hymns and sermons as 'Narcotics'? Like a drug, they have the ability to pacify momentarily, have a numbing effect which might ease pain in one way. However, as Dickinson claims in her final vivid and discomforting image, they 'cannot still the Tooth / That nibbles at the soul –'. It might be too much to expect Dickinson to have been aware of Karl Marx's **metaphorical** description, in his 1844 *Critique of the Hegelian Philosophy of Right*, of religion as the opium of the people, but she clearly had much the same thought.

512 The soul has bandaged moments – 1862 (1945)

A description of the Soul's moments of restraint and freedom

The Soul has moments when it feels constrained, restricted, and assaulted by some horrors. The soul also has moments of freedom. These moments end, however, and the soul, like an escaped criminal, is recaptured.

This poem is divided into three sections, each containing two stanzas, and each section describes a condition of the soul. The first two stanzas suggest constraint, restriction, and a violation of the soul, which seems very much like a rape, by some 'ghastly Fright' that remains unidentified, and who caresses her and kisses the lips that previously her lover had kissed. The third and fourth stanzas celebrate the moments when the soul is free from such constraints; the sense of freedom experienced is compared to the feelings of a bee which has been forbidden but finally allowed access to the rose. The last two stanzas describe the moment of recapture, when the soul is again put under restraint and, like an escaped criminal, taken back to meet the 'Horror'. These are the moments about which the soul does not sing.

This poem contains one of Dickinson's most shocking and effective first lines. Although Dickinson is talking about the condition of a soul, her ideas are conveyed in an extremely concrete and visual form. What kind of a visual image is presented by the idea of the soul having 'Bandaged moments'? The **image** is suggestive of perhaps someone hurt, damaged, whose wounds have been wrapped in bandages, but it also suggests restraint, as though the soul is bound up. Her inability to move, however, is the result of being 'too appalled' by the 'ghastly Fright' coming up and assaulting her. She is so appalled, afraid, that her very hair is 'freezing', indicative of the sudden chill of fear, but additionally emphasising the rigid, petrified state of the soul. Why does this assault seem very much like a kind of rape? There is something rather distasteful, even menacing, about the long fingers fondling her and sipping from her lips, with the word 'Sip' suggesting he is slowly savouring the assault. Do you think the dashes and the internal rhyme in the line 'The Lover – hovered – o'er' slow down the pace momentarily, perhaps imitating the slow hovering of the lover himself?

The description of the soul's moments of escape in the middle two stanzas are also presented in highly visual terms. Now we see the power that has previously been restrained: 'bursting all the doors', she 'dances like a Bomb, abroad'. What is the effect of this **simile**? A bomb contains energy which is potentially destructive, and so has negative connotations. However, she 'dances': there is freedom and delight and self-expression here, and this is emphasised by the way she 'swings upon the Hours', making the most of every moment. This image of the soul's moments of escape is developed with another simile, drawn from the natural world. What does it suggest about the bee that it should, once it gains access to the rose, 'know no more, / but Noon, and Paradise –'. Both noon and paradise imply complete fulfilment and satisfaction.

In the next stanza the soul has been recaptured. Again we have a very visual image to convey the restraint which is reimposed: she is a 'Felon led along'. The feet which were 'plumed', feathered, that is, as though she were a bird, are now in 'shackles', as though she were a criminal. How do you respond to the image of 'staples, in the Song'? How can something aural, as intangible as a song, be stapled, staples being used to secure something, pin something down. It is a very appropriate way of describing the restraint of something as abstract as a soul. So far the poem has progressed primarily in stanzas of four lines, with the exception of stanza two, where the extended lines could be said to enact the long savouring sipping assault of the goblin. Now, however, the poem concludes with a stanza of only two lines as 'The Horror welcomes her, again'. These moments 'are not brayed of Tongue –' the poem is cut off short with two lines, much like the Soul's song is cut off; the horrors she will now experience will not even be 'brayed of Tongue –'. What is the contrast suggested by singing and braying? A bray is a long harsh sound, usually associated with a donkey. Not only will the soul no longer sing, now shackled once more, she is not even able to complain of this: she is silenced, repressed.

585 I LIKE TO SEE IT LAP THE MILES – 1862 (1891)

A description of a railway locomotive

The locomotive devours everything in its path. It finally arrives at its destination docile as a horse returning to its stable. It is described making its way through the valleys, around mountains, and down hills; it appears as a monstrous creature devouring everything in its path. At the end of its journey, however, it loses all its energy and power, stopping docile as a horse at its stable door.

This playful lyric poses a **riddle** to the reader: what is the 'it' which is described? The controlling **metaphor** is the railway locomotive as the 'iron horse', the name given to trains when they first appeared in the nineteenth century. Dickinson never uses the words 'railway locomotive' with reference to the object she describes. What textual evidence, therefore, identifies the object? One clue can be found in the **onomatopoeic** effect created by the choice of consonants in the first few lines; reading these lines out loud will emphasise the locomotive sound produced by l-k-l-p-l-k. The entire poem consists of one long compound sentence which helps to convey a sense of movement and direction, and this is further emphasised by the accumulation of action verbs and the **enjambed** lines. The regularity of the first two stanzas establishes the sense of a steady pace which is emphasised by the **alliterative** effects. This sense of regularity is then disrupted in the third stanza by variations in **metre** and line length when the locomotive is suddenly faced with more difficult terrain. No longer superciliously peering in the ramshackle dwellings it passes, it becomes a hooting monster which complains as it must 'fit its Ribs' and crawl along. Perhaps Dickinson herself could be said here to create her own 'horrid – hooting stanza' in some way. A sense of sudden speed is then suggested as the locomotive goes down hill, only to end in the final stanza with an abrupt 'Stop'. What is the effect of the **spondee** in this penultimate line? How does this help sound to convey meaning? The locomotive now seems transformed into a docile horse.

Do you think that, overall, this poem conveys the sense of excitement caused by the appearance of the train in the nineteenth century, or do you think it offers some pessimistic commentary on the potentially negative impact of the industrial society the train represents? The playfulness of the poem should be set against the negative implications of such words as 'horrid' and 'Shanties'. These shanties might be the dwellings of those who build the railways; what effect might this industrial development have had on their lives? Furthermore, while the locomotive is ultimately described as 'docile', and therefore apparently harmless, it is also described as 'omnipotent', and therefore possessing ultimate power. In what way could this be a criticism of industry?

Boanerges 'sons of thunder'. The name given to James and John, sons of Zebeddee, who wanted to call down fire from heaven to consume the Samaritans for not receiving Jesus. Luke 9:54; Mark 3:17

640 **I** CANNOT LIVE WITH YOU –   1862 (1890)

The renunciation of love

The speaker considers life, death and resurrection in turn, and decides that she could not be with her lover in any of these situations and so they must remain apart.

In this, Dickinson's longest poem and one of her most poignant love **lyrics**, the speaker proceeds by identifying the reasons why she and her lover cannot live together. It would be, she claims, life, and life is what they are not allowed to experience in the world of regulation and restraint. In the third stanza she says they cannot die together either, since one must remain to perform the last offices for the other: he would be unable to do this – he could not do it – for her, and she could not bear to see him die without her. Nor can they be together at the moment of resurrection: as she says in stanzas six and seven, her idolatrous love would prevent her from accepting Christ. In the afterlife, if they were separated, she would be in Hell whether she was the one lost or saved. The only option that remains is for them to stay apart.

This poem combines two different **tones**. There is the formal tone of the repeated lines of renunciation which take on the features of a catechism: 'I cannot live with You –', 'I could not die – with You –' and so on, which divide the thought structure of the poem. There is also the more colloquial and conversational tone which enters as the speaker explains to her lover why she cannot do these things. The language throughout, however, remains tightly controlled; this may be an expression of despair, of anguish, but no sentimentality enters the poem. The repeated use of dashes creates a sense of tension, as though emotion is being held in. And this feeling of tight restraint is further effected by the short lines, the highly compressed use of language and the use of listing, which suggests progression. The poem is organised as though it were presenting a logical argument: the anguished emotions consequently appear as though they were rationalised and objectified.

The first three stanzas of this poem, linked by the use of **enjambment**, focus upon why the speaker and her lover cannot live together: 'It would be Life – / And Life is over there –'. Through this **paradoxical** statement, it becomes clear that what the speaker has cannot be described as 'Life' as she would define it. There may be echoes here of Heathcliff saying of Cathy: 'I *cannot* live without my life' in Emily Brontë's *Wuthering Heights*, the basic passionate paradox being much the same. A highly complex sequence of **images** follows. Life is something kept locked up by the Sexton. The use of the term 'Sexton' suggests that there is some religious prohibition; a certain kind of living is imposed upon them which prohibits their fulfilment. In turn, this life locked up by the sexton is described in terms of domestic imagery. The Sexton locks up 'Our life – His Porcelain – / Like a Cup –'; while initially there may be a suggestion of a communion cup, of the sacrament of the Last Supper, this cup becomes one 'Discarded of the Housewife' because it is 'Quaint – or Broke –'. The domestic imagery repeatedly overtakes the religious.

In the next two stanzas, also linked by enjambment, she describes why she cannot die with him. Dying might carry the faint association of sexual fulfilment (to die is a familiar **metaphor** for sexual climax), but the stress is more upon the literal act of dying. He 'could not' attend her death, the reason is left unstated. She would be unable to attend his. A cry of pain at the very thought emerges in the way the **assonantal** 'i' sound dominates this line 'And I – Could I stand by'.

She could not give up her 'Right of Frost'; if he died she too would have to die.

Nor, she says in the next two linked stanzas as the poem moves from earth to paradise, could she rise, go to heaven, with him: 'Your face / Would put out Jesus". The idea of the lover eclipsing Christ continues as she considers how they would be judged after death. He at least sought to serve Heaven while she could not: 'Because You saturated Sight –'. He took up all her vision. Even Paradise appears but a 'sordid excellence' in comparison to him, while Hell, as she observes in the next two stanzas, is not something to which she would be condemned by God's judgement; hell would be defined by the lover's absence.

'So', the poem concludes, they must 'meet apart'. How can two people meet apart? The emphasis must be on an emotional rather than a physical connection. 'You there – I – here –'. The very dashes in this line insist upon separation and distance. 'With just the Door ajar / That Oceans are –'. What might this suggest about the distance that they must keep from each other? It is minimal, as though they were on two sides of an open door, but it is distance and any distance makes her feel as though they are oceans apart. Why is the sustenance she now survives on, despair, described as 'White'? Whiteness suggests purification, but also perhaps sterility. It has been suggested that this 'White Sustenance' might have associations with manna, the food provided for the Israelites by God on their journey from Egypt to the Holy Land (Exodus 16:31). If so, this is a different kind of manna, not a promise of future fulfilment, but a thin comfort drained of any real nourishment: despair is all she will have. It has also been claimed there is a sense of calm acceptance in this final stanza. This could be partly the effect of the stress falling on that first word 'So': the argument is summed up, the conclusion reached. Is any particular effect created by the addition of two extra lines to this stanza? Could they perhaps formally enact the growing space between the lovers? Is it possible they even insist upon it? This poem could be usefully compared with 'There came a Day at Summer's full' (322), which, although similarly concerned with the separation of two lovers, anticipates fulfilment in heaven.

Sexton caretaker of church and graveyard
Sevres porcelain manufactured at Sèvres, near Paris

668 'NATURE' IS WHAT WE SEE – 1863 (1914)

An attempt to define nature

The poem is divided into three sections. The first claims nature is what we see; the second that nature is what we hear; the third that nature is what we know but cannot express.

This poem takes the form of a dialogue between two voices. In the first four lines, the first voice says that Nature is what we see, what we apprehend with our senses: 'The Hill – the Afternoon – / Squirrel – Eclipse – the Bumble bee –'. The second voice comes in at the fourth line: 'Nay – Nature is Heaven –'. The next four lines offer a parallel construction. The first voice now draws upon another of the senses, hearing: Nature, it now claims, is 'The Bobolink – / the Sea – / Thunder – the Cricket –'. Again the second voice responds: 'Nay, Nature is Harmony –'. In the final four lines it is not clear who is speaking: it could be a third voice, or a combination of the first two: 'Nature is what we know – / Yet have no art to say –'. This time, no voice corrects the assertion.

> The difference between the two voices in the first eight lines is that one represents the concrete and material approach to nature: it focuses upon externals and lists things large and small. The other represents the abstract approach: it expresses itself not through specifics, nor externals, but in larger, more comprehensive terms. Some critics would say that this poem represents an attempt to define nature in **Transcendental** terms, that Emerson's notions of nature as the great teacher, as something we read, as the source of moral wisdom, are echoed here. But do you think this point is actually expressed here without reservation?

In 'Nature is what we know – / Yet have no art to say –' a distinction is made between perception and expression. The point of the poem itself is to attempt definition, to attempt to express what nature is, but here the speaker suggests this is what we cannot do. Why are we unable to 'say' what nature is? The concluding lines might offer an explanation: 'So impotent Our Wisdom is / To her Simplicity'. Why would nature be ultimately described in terms of 'her Simplicity'? This quality contrasts with the multiplicity of her external manifestations, all the specific details that the eye and ear can apprehend, define, and name. 'Nature', however, in its larger abstract sense, eludes us. The attempt to give meaning, to exert any control over nature is made 'impotent' by 'her Simplicity'. For a discussion of Dickinson's perspective on nature, see Themes, on Nature.

Bobolink an American songbird

670 ONE NEED NOT BE A CHAMBER – TO BE HAUNTED – 1863 (1891)

The dangers of confrontations within the mind

The mind can be haunted as well as a physical space can be. The dangers we encounter in Gothic castles are, in fact, 'far safer', than the dangers we might find in the mind.

The poem develops a **metaphorical** comparison between two kinds of dwellings and two varieties of haunting. The mind is here described as a physical space, a dwelling space with corridors and chambers. Both the second and third stanzas assert that the frightening events of **Gothic** castles and abbeys, encounters with ghosts and assassins, are 'Far safer' than the kind of events that might occur in the mind. The body might protect itself by taking up a weapon and bolting the door, but the mind will soon discover it has only locked itself in with 'a superior spectre – / Or More –'.

This is one of many poems in which Dickinson describes a mental experience in more concrete terms, here drawing upon the plots of Gothic romances. Do you think that Dickinson manages to create quite a chilling effect in this poem? If so, how is this done? There is a great deal of repetition, which in itself might create a sense of haunting, echoing. Why should we be 'Far safer' with ghosts and assassins than with the horrors we might encounter within our minds? This is partly, it seems, because within the mind one is 'Unarmed'. We are prepared to find dangers in Gothic castles; we are not prepared for the internal dangers, the confrontations with the self.

Does that final **exact rhyme**, combined with the brevity of the final two-syllable line, create quite an ominous effect? Does the use of the final dash, in addition, undercut **closure** and suggest that something is just about to happen?

712 BECAUSE I COULD NOT STOP FOR DEATH — 1863 (1890)

Death as a gentleman caller takes the speaker for a ride in his carriage

The speaker tells us about her encounter with Death. Death is **personified**, presented as a proper gentleman caller who stops by to take the speaker for a ride in his carriage. Since this is the mid nineteenth century, there must be a chaperone: this is Immortality. The speaker describes what she sees out of the window. She begins to feel cold. The house to which death brings her, like a bridegroom conducting his bride to a new home, is a fresh grave. Here, however, they only pause; their ultimate destination lies further on. Moving to the present tense the speaker then reflects back on the moment she first realised she was moving toward 'Eternity'.

The speaker begins with a rather shocking announcement – one of Dickinson's many dislocating first lines – but expresses herself in a quite understated, even casual tone. We might expect Death to be talked about using words that convey fear, or awe, but not here. He is a charming and courteous nineteenth-century gentleman caller. What aspects of the description of the experience further contribute to the presentation of this encounter as a pleasant social occasion? Does the speaker seem willing to go for the ride with Death? Do you find any significant details in the description of the journey? Stanza three, where the speaker describes what she sees out of the window, is particularly suggestive. If this were just an ordinary carriage drive, we might take these lines literally. But it is more than this. Dickinson is using the idea of the drive out with the gentleman caller in a **metaphorical** manner, and since this is an encounter with death these lines take on additional meaning. First there is the schoolyard, with children playing; then there are fields of grain, and finally the setting sun. What we have here is a series of stages: the concrete details of the scene metaphorically describe in a highly compressed manner the progression of life: from youth, the children, to maturity, the ripe grain, to old age, sunset. The sunset is like the border between life and death. The **anaphoric** repetition of 'We passed' in this stanza emphasises that some boundary is being crossed, and that the speaker is moving towards a place which is outside time and change.

It is useful at this point to consider the **metre** of the poem. Despite the fact that death is being described, the poem has a pleasant soothing, regular rhythm, promoting a peaceful effect. But there is one very significant variation. If you scan the first lines of each stanza you will find that every first line, with the exception of that in stanza four, is written in **iambic tetrameter;** the first line in stanza four is irregular, disruptive, and we need to ask if this irregularity is functional. With the change from a four- to a three-stress line Dickinson seems to be signalling to us that another kind of change is taking place: that there is a move into another plane of existence, into perhaps death. We have had sunset, and now: 'The Dews drew quivering and chill'; a sense of damp and cold is emphasised by the use of **alliteration** and by the icy sharp 'i' sounds. The speaker explains the chill she feels to be the result of her light clothing, but it is surely the coldness associated with death: she has become as cold as a corpse.

In the next stanza, the regular rhythm returns, but the serene and casual tone is lost. The house to which death brings her, like a bridegroom conducting his bride to a new home, is a fresh grave. Now, in the final stanza, she abruptly turns from the past to the present tense, suggesting that she has been looking back on a previous experience; the speaker is dead, she has been speaking to us from Eternity. The poem concludes with a dash, here, highly functional, as it implies no definite **closure**, no end. Is this then a positive ending, suggesting that death leads to immortality? Alternately, can it be read in a more negative fashion? There is no sense here of a peaceful union after death with some divine being, just a sense of loss, of timeless separation from life. Compare this with another poem in which Dickinson depicts death as a courtly suitor but with a slightly more sinister touch: 'Death is the supple Suitor' (1445) (see Themes, on Death).

Gossamer a thin gauze or silk fabric
Tippet a cape or short cloak

Tulle a fine net fabric

Cornice plaster moulding at the top of a wall or building

732 SHE ROSE TO HIS REQUIREMENTS – DROPT 1863 (1890)

The negative and positive aspects of marriage for women

A woman gives up the life of unthinking pleasure associated with childhood to take on the role of wife. The speaker reflects upon the regrets the woman might have, regrets which, if they occur, must be buried and unspoken.

Is this an entirely negative assessment of marriage from the woman's perspective, or does the speaker reveal a certain ambivalence?

Dickinson alternates between using words suggestive of positive values and words with negative values. In the first stanza, the work of woman and wife is described as 'honorable', and to take on this work she drops the 'Playthings' of her life. What are the implications of the use of the word 'Playthings', with its associations of childhood. And yet the woman gives up her childish pleasures at 'His Requirement'. Does this introduce any negative element?

There is repeatedly a sense that what the woman gains is offset by what the woman loses, but which is emphasised? The word 'rose' is offset by 'dropt'; which word gains the most emphasis and why? Remember that the poet has the choice of where to place the line breaks. Compare this with the implications of that concluding image of the sea developing both 'Pearl' and 'Weed'. This **analogy** between woman and sea suggests that if the woman misses anything in her new life, she keeps her feelings hidden within, and what is produced as a result may be as positive as a pearl or as negative as a weed.

Do you think the poem ultimately emphasises what the woman loses, or what the woman gains, through marriage? Perhaps all we can say is that this poem provides a good example of how Dickinson recognised that marriage, for a nineteenth-century woman, was both a positive move, in that it represented a movement into adulthood, and a negative, in that it nevertheless reinstated another childlike state by denying her an individual identity (see Themes, on Love & Marriage).

747 IT DROPPED SO LOW – IN MY REGARD – 1863 (1896)

The loss of respect for something once valued

Something once highly valued drops in the speaker's regard and smashes like a piece of 'plated ware' upon the ground. She blames herself for valuing something essentially not worth her regard.

This is one of Dickinson's many poems in which she talks about an 'it' which is ultimately unidentified. The central **metaphor** she uses is of a piece of ordinary pottery dropping to the ground and smashing. If the pottery is the *vehicle* or the metaphor, however, what is the *tenor* – that is, what does the pottery refer us to? 'It' is obviously something far more significant than a simple piece of broken pottery. A physical event is being used to describe a mental experience.

The second stanza suggests that what was most painful about this experience was that it was her own fault; it is not that she has been deceived by someone or something, but that she has deceived herself. The speaker blames herself for the fall. 'It' is metaphorically described as 'Plated Wares' that the speaker has placed upon her 'Silver Shelf'. What does this tell us about 'It'; does it suggest that 'It' has not been worthy of being so well treated, that the crash has been her fault because she has overestimated the value of 'It'? Do you think it is clear what the referent of 'It' is by the end of the poem? Do we really need to pin 'It' down to something specific?

754 MY LIFE HAD STOOD – A LOADED GUN – 1863 (1929)

A metaphorical description of the speaker's life as a gun, serving her 'Master'

In the first stanza the speaker describes her life as a loaded gun, unused, until the owner identifies it and takes it away. She then describes their life together as they hunt; she serves him, guarding him at night. She is a deadly foe to any of his enemies. Though she may live longer than he, he must live longer than she. The explanation: 'For I have but the power to kill, / Without – the power to die –'.

The opening line offers a **metaphor** which fuses together the abstract and the concrete: a gun becomes the *vehicle* for the *tenor* of the speaker's life. It is a dislocating, disturbing opening line: there appears to be such disparity between a life and a loaded gun. Rather than try to explain the disparities, however, the poem moves on to develop the story. From this point onwards, the speaker's life is never mentioned and the poem works purely on the level of the vehicle of that metaphor. A series of metaphors then considers gunfire from the gun's perspective, emphasising the delight and the beauty of gunfire. When the gun speaks for the owner, it appears to the gun that 'The Mountains straight reply'; this is, of course, from our perspective, the gun shots echoing back. The moment of explosive violence seems satisfying, pleasurable. 'And do I smile', for example, she says in stanza three, 'such cordial light / Upon the Valley glow' that it is as though 'a Vesuvian face / Had let its pleasure through –'. In this example, when the gun smiles, that is, fires, the light that emerges is first described as 'cordial'; cordial, that is, warm and friendly, seems a strange description for the result of gunfire. The **image** is then further complicated with a **simile** which compares this light to the eruption of a volcano, a volcano that 'Had let its pleasure through –'. Again, the eruption of a volcano, something violent and destructive, is described in positive terms. Do you think that under some circumstances allowing oneself to erupt violently might indeed be pleasurable? Could it allow for the release of feelings that have been tightly restrained?

The **tone** of delight, of intense pleasure, is partly created through the **anaphoric** use of 'And', the repetition conveying a sense of growing excitement, and also a, surely deceptive, sense of growing control. The gun moves from seeing itself as the passive object 'carried' away by an owner in stanza one, to seeing itself as able to act, but only at his demand in stanza two where 'I speak for Him', to ultimately seeing itself as in complete control in stanza five, where even the thumb which pulls the triggers appears as its own.

Various interpretation have been offered concerning the identity of gun and owner and the nature of the experience described. One interpretation describes the experience as that of falling in love; the poem demonstrates how by losing oneself in love one can **paradoxically** achieve identity: the owner 'identified' her: she achieves identity when he claims her for his own. Expanding upon this, we might say that this is a nonsexual relationship: the gun prefers guarding the master to sharing his bed, prefers violence to sexuality. Another interpretation suggests the gun stands for those aspects of the speaker's character that have been socially and culturally associated with the masculine, and to achieve the power she does involves, in a **patriarchal** society, the sacrifice of her feminine side. Notably, the only figure in the poem directly identified as female is the doe: that must be hunted and killed. Furthermore, sharing the man's bed is rejected in favour of guarding it; the speaker is denying all conventional female roles. Another **feminist** interpretation suggests that the poem demonstrates the woman writer's appropriation of male power. While he is the one who has carried her away, she is the one who acts. We could also see the owner/master as God, and the gun as a representative of the human beings he uses as instruments of his will. They, of course, believe themselves to be in complete control, their power their own, as the gun claims in stanza five when it seems to think that even the 'emphatic Thumb' which pulls the trigger is its own.

All these interpretative possibilities, however, seem confounded by the paradox of the final four lines. The **aphoristic** nature of these lines suggests something is being summed up, concluded, explained. But what? Perhaps it is less like an aphorism than a **riddle**. But, if so, what is the answer? As many critics have observed, it is a particularly puzzling stanza. The lines claim that the gun may live longer than the owner, but that he *must* nevertheless live longer than the gun: 'For I have but the power to kill, / Without – the power to die –'. On the level of the vehicle of the metaphor this might make sense: a gun can indeed kill but not die. We might be tempted to conclude that the gun is, after all, nothing more than a gun, but this would be to ignore the opening line: the gun is a metaphor for the speaker's life. How can the final stanza, though, possibly be applied to human beings; how can they have the power to kill without the power to die? No satisfactory explanation of these lines has been offered so far. The poem suggests a multiplicity of possible interpretations, but then confounds them all. The claim of that final stanza prevents us from associating the gun with a life, but the metaphor which drives the poem simultaneously insists that we keep trying.

Vesuvian Vesuvius is a volcano in Italy; its first recorded eruption, in AD 79, destroyed Pompeii
Eider-Duck species of duck, the female of which is the source of eiderdown

986 A NARROW FELLOW IN THE GRASS 1865 (1866)

A description of a snake and the fascination and fear it can induce

The speaker describes the snake with reference to how it looks and the habitat it prefers and recalls a boyhood encounter with a snake. The snake is the only one of nature's creatures that causes terror in the speaker.

At first, the snake is described riding through the grass. The speaker then recalls how, when a boy, he nearly picked up a snake sunning itself when he mistook it for a whip. The poem ends with a comparison between the cordial feeling the speaker has for other natural creatures and the terror that the snake inspires in him. The word snake, however, is never used.

Like 'I like to see it lap the Miles –' (585), this poem offers us a **riddle** to solve: what is this 'narrow Fellow'? The solution here may be easy to guess, but it is useful to consider how Dickinson suggests the idea of the snake and the speaker's attitude towards it.

The first stanza conveys the idea of a snake primarily through the **alliterative** 's' which echoes the creature's hiss. From this aural suggestion we move to the visual images created by 'spotted shaft' and 'Whip lash'. Finally, the speaker conveys what we could call the essence of 'snakeness' by describing its effect upon him. For many creatures, he feels a 'transport / Of cordiality' – a phrase which rather comically combines overstated ecstasy with formal restraint. The rather playful tone, however, radically changes with the final lines.

This 'Fellow' he never meets: 'Without a tighter breathing / And Zero at the Bone –'. There is a sudden constriction in breathing and a hollow, numbing coldness emphasised by the chilling **assonance** of the final phrase. In what sense can Dickinson's use of rhyme in this poem be said to convey a sense of movement towards this moment of climactic intensity when the speaker feels 'Zero at the Bone'? If you examine the rhyme scheme you will find that there is a movement from **slant rhyme** to **exact rhyme** and that final strong and exact rhyme of 'alone' and 'Bone' which stands out so emphatically brings a sudden end to the light and discursive tone which precedes it. The snake is biblically and traditionally associated with evil; do you think this association plays any part here or is it just a simple poem about one of nature's creatures? If the latter, then why should the snake have this effect upon the speaker? For a discussion of Dickinson's perspective on nature, see Themes, on Nature.

1072 TITLE DIVINE – IS MINE! 1862 (1924)

The speaker celebrates her achievement in being a 'wife' without the normal trappings of wifehood. The two kinds of 'marriage' are compared

The poem begins with the speaker's exclamation of delight at her achievement: she has the 'Title divine'. This is then defined as the title of wife, but wife 'without the Sign!'; she is not, that is, wife in the ordinary way. A series of phrases then attempt to define further her way of being 'wife', each associating her state with divinity and royalty. In attempting to define her own particular state of wifehood, the speaker describes what she does and does not possess. She is, for example, 'The Wife – without the Sign!', 'Royal – all but the Crown!', and 'Betrothed – without the swoon'. As these lines suggest, what primarily defines her state is that although exalted, divine, royal, she possesses none of the external signs which usually define these qualities.

This is one of the poems which most clearly demonstrates how Dickinson can create effects of great intensity with the use of compression. There is not one superfluous word. This does, of course, contribute to the difficulty of the poem. What kind of 'marriage' do you think the speaker is celebrating? Some critics see the speaker as a bride of Christ; others believe she is describing the special kind of 'marriage' that she has and comparing this to the more common earthly marriages. The language of the poem draws upon both secular and spiritual love. The Christian language, however, does not necessarily mean she is seeing herself as the bride of Christ; she may simply be using this language to convey her sense of the profound and very special nature of her relationship.

How does Dickinson create the celebratory tone in this opening section? To begin with, the poem is punctuated throughout with exclamations which convey the speaker's exultation. Some critics, it should be added, have suggested these exclamation marks are rather excessive, and wonder if it is simply exultation that is being expressed or if there is a rather disturbing shrill intensity about these lines. The celebratory tone is also created by the way the lines are divided frequently by dashes which create strong **caesuras**, adding weight and emphasis to her pronouncements; initially the caesuras also help with the comparison, with the first half of the line defining what she has, and the second half indicating the external signs of this that she does not have: a sense of triumph is also conveyed by the opening **rhyming couplets** which, again, add weight and finality to each pronouncement.

The poem becomes more difficult to pin down in lines eight and nine. When is it that you 'hold – Garnet to Garnet – / Gold to Gold'? This could be read as referring back to 'without the swoon', and suggesting that women swoon at the marriage ceremony when they exchange rings with their husbands. She, however, has not had this ceremony, nor does she have the ring and, therefore, nor has she had the swoon. It is not clear how the next three lines fit in with this. Who is 'Born – Bridalled – Shrouded – / In a Day'; who has this 'Tri Victory'? The words are packed with possible meanings apart from the literal. 'Born' could also indicate what a wife has 'borne'; 'bridalled' could suggest both confinement and restraint, and yet also that she might 'bridle' at being 'bridled'. 'Shrouded' seems particularly negative: as one critic suggests the birth of the wife is the death of the individual woman. Consequently, the lines could refer to the ordinary wives. If so, there is some **irony** in the claim that this is a 'Tri Victory'. It is the speaker who is associated with death and resurrection, however, when she describes herself as 'Empress of Calvary' and so perhaps the 'Tri Victory' belongs to her. Since the poem as a whole is offering a strong endorsement of the speaker's kind of marriage, it would surely be her, the wife with the 'Title divine' who has any victory. The concluding lines are equally **ambiguous**. They have been alternatively read as the speaker expressing contempt for women who are in a more conventional kind of marriage, and the speaker moving away from distinguishing herself from other women to underlining her affinity with them. How would you read the final three lines? It is useful to try to establish what you think the **tone** might be here before deciding if Dickinson is contemptuous of ordinary women or declaring her affinity with them. Consider in particular the wonderful and quite erotic image of the wife 'Stroking the Melody' – can one touch something as abstract as a melody? What is meant by the rather coy, even coquettish question 'Is *this* – the way?' The way to what – to behave perhaps, to win love? Do you think these final lines offer a disdainful assessment of how common wives behave, or is it the 'wife' with the 'Title Divine' who is now identifying herself with women generally?

Calvary the place outside the walls of Jerusalem where Jesus was crucified; a calvary can refer to any representation of Christ's crucifixion and even, more generally, to any experience involving great suffering
Garnet red gemstone which represents constancy

1100 THE LAST NIGHT THAT SHE LIVED 1866 (1890)

A woman's death and its effects upon the observers

The speaker recalls the night when a woman was dying. Those observing wait in silence as she dies; they then make the necessary adjustments to the dead body and are left to try to reconcile their religious beliefs with the death of a loved one.

Recalling the night on which a woman died, the speaker remembers how the presence of death made everything different: the ordinary became extraordinary, and things previously unnoticed became of great significance. Their activity, coming and going between rooms, is contrasted with her passivity, as she waits for death. The third and fourth stanzas describe the varying responses of those who are waiting and observing: they are both angered that she should die while others less worthy live on, and yet also envy the dying woman because they must continue to suffer life's pains. The woman dies peacefully as they watch; they prepare the dead body and then are left with nothing more to do save attempt to reconcile their religious beliefs with the fact that this loved woman has died.

Why should the fact of an imminent death change one's perspective on the world? Why should the smallest thing become 'Italicized'? It could be because a reminder of mortality causes us to value much more what we have. What kind of visual **image** is offered by the **simile** which compares the dying woman with a 'Reed'? A reed is slender, fragile, bent by the winds, and the woman too gives in to death with little struggle. The image could be said to emphasise our fragility, our mortality. After death, the woman is reduced to parts, to 'the Hair' and to the 'Head'. There seems to be little to individualise her now. It has been suggested that the verbal style of this **lyric** creates a sense of rigidly controlled hysteria. Would you agree, or would you say the **tone** is calm and reflective?

1670 **I**N WINTER IN MY ROOM ? (1914)

The power of sexual attraction and the fear and repulsion that such attraction may arouse

A woman finds in her room a worm; it seems harmless, but she is not comfortable with it and tries to secure it with a piece of string. When she returns to her room, the worm has been replaced by a powerful snake. There is a dialogue between the woman and the snake: she tries to appease it, but the snake advances. She runs away to a distant town and the poem ends with the claim that this was all a dream.

This poem proceeds in four stanzas which, if you consider their literal shape upon the page, with their varying line lengths, in themselves create quite a serpentine shape. We are first introduced to the setting, a room in wintertime. Why should Dickinson open this poem in winter: what associations does winter have for us: coldness, perhaps, sterility? The speaker discovers a worm, 'Pink lank and warm', seemingly harmless, but, of course, also exceedingly phallic. The worm may seem harmless, but 'worms presume'. How they presume is left unclear. Uneasy, therefore – as one might be – the speaker ties the worm up with a piece of string. In the second stanza the speaker tells us what happened soon afterwards: the worm had changed into a snake, 'ringed with power'. Stanza three opens with dialogue, although it is unclear to whom the words should be assigned. The phallic **imagery** of stanza three culminates in an image of sexual climax. Terrified, the woman runs away to a 'distant Town' and the firm claim from the speaker: 'This was a dream.'

A poem like this, it has been said by some critics, could have been written only before Freud. After Freud everyone would be too aware of the potential sexual suggestions to write with quite the same lack of self-consciousness we find here about pink lank worms which cause fear and repulsion. A **psychoanalytical** reading of this poem would focus upon its revelation of repressed desire. This would probably not involve reading the dialogue in stanza three as an exchange between woman and snake; instead, the woman could be seen to shrink from the snake while he tries to seduce her: all the dialogue could be assigned to the snake. It is equally possible, however, that while the woman shrinks away she is also attracted, and that she is the one who says 'How fair you are'! Who speaks remains **ambiguous**. There is little ambiguity, however, about the description of the snake first fathoming, that is, penetrating, the speaker, and then 'to a Rhythm *Slim* / Secreted in his Form / As Patterns swim / Projected him'; this is, as many critics have pointed out, a clear indication of penetration and climax. If we take the feelings provoked by the snake to suggest repressed desire, then the firm claim of the conclusion that 'This was a dream' would be seen as the conscious mind, the ego, rejecting the drives of the subconscious id.

However, we need to be careful about concluding that this poem reveals Dickinson's own fears of male sexuality, and equally careful about deciding she was not aware of what she was suggesting. Remember the first line of the last stanza: 'That time I flew': *that* time, but, the implication seems to be, not every time. It is even quite possible to see Dickinson aiming for a comic effect in this poem, as Martha Nell Smith has argued: try to visualise the speaker here running backwards, with both eyes towards the snake (in *Comic Power in Emily Dickinson*, eds. Suzanne Juhasz et al., p. 98). And what about the completely ridiculous image of the speaker tying up the worm with a piece of string; why not throw it outside? Compare the attitude towards sexuality in this **lyric** with such lyrics as 'Did the Harebell loose her girdle' (213) and 'Wild Nights – Wild Nights!' (249) to see how Dickinson can move from playfulness to eroticism. Do you think it is significant that Dickinson should so consistently draw upon imagery from the natural world to suggest sexuality? If you compare these lyrics with the lyrics about marriage, you will see that in the marriage poems this natural imagery generally disappears.

PART THREE

CRITICAL APPROACHES

THEMES

DEATH

Dickinson's concern with death, which may initially appear morbid to the twentieth-century reader, needs to be understood within the context of her time. There was the constant threat of tuberculosis; what we might consider common unimportant illnesses today, such as pneumonia, then often led to death; even pregnancy and childbirth were far more dangerous than they are now. Furthermore, as Barton Levi St Armand has most notably shown in *Emily Dickinson and Her Culture*, Dickinson's fascination with death was a response to many of the concerns of her culture, including deathbed watches, highly ritualistic funerals, and mementoes of the dying, such as the mourning jewellery that frequently incorporated the hair of the loved one – all the iconography of romanticised death and mourning. There was also a fashion for mortuary poetry, such as Mrs C.W. Hunt's 'Georgiana', which includes such lines as:

> She lay within her coffin-cell
> Like a priceless pearl in costly shell,
> Enshrined in light, so pure – so rare,
> A breath would leave a shadow there. (qouted in St Armand)

You may be more familiar with such poetry from the satiric description of Emmeline Grangerford's mawkish deathbed lyrics in *Huckleberry Finn*. All these things seem very distant and alien to our society, where death has become rather a taboo, ignored as much as possible, but they were very much part of Dickinson's world. Not that Dickinson is sentimental about death; she appropriates the paraphernalia of her cultural traditions, but submits them, as St Armand demonstrates, to her techniques of domestication, exaggeration and inversion. Even the traditional religious view of death as a peaceful release from the pain of life and the reward of immortality is questioned. Such ideas are treated **ironically** in, for example, 'I heard a Fly buzz – when I died –' (465 – see Extended

Commentaries, Text 2); those watching the dying speaker are anticipating 'that last Onset – when the King / Be witnessed – in the Room –'. But all that happens is that 'There interposed a Fly –', an ordinary buzzing housefly. The fly, the corruption of the body, is perhaps all that awaits us after death, the poem suggests. Dickinson thoroughly explores every aspect of death in her poetry. She considers the physical, the psychological and the emotional aspects of this unknowable experience. She considers, for example, the bodily changes at the moment of death in 'I like a look of Agony' (241), the effects of someone dying on the observers in 'The last Night that she Lived' (1100). She looks at death from the perspective of both the living and the dying, even imagining her own death. Death is frequently personified; he is the courteous gentleman caller in 'Because I could not stop for Death' (712) and the deceptive seducer in 'Death is the supple Suitor'(1445). Death is the one completely unknowable experience, and Dickinson devotes much of her poetry to imagining his many faces.

LOVE & MARRIAGE

Many critics have tried to find a love affair in Dickinson's life to account for the numerous poems she wrote about love. The interest in Dickinson's own relationships was intensified by the discovery of love letters addressed to an unidentified 'Master'. She has been linked with many men, including two married men who were basically unaware of her feelings, and various women, most notably her brother's wife Susan. Some feminist critics have persuasively argued for the presence of a homoerotic strain in Dickinson's work.

A number of Dickinson's poems about love and sexual relationships reveal a playful, even flirtatious tone. Examples would include 'Did the Harebell loose her girdle' (213), and 'The Daisy follows soft the Sun –' (106). While such poems as these are playfully erotic, there are other Dickinson poems, focusing on the physical aspects of desire, in which the tone is highly sensuous, including 'Come slowly – Eden! (211) and 'Wild Nights – Wild Nights! (249 – see Extended Commentaries, Text 3), which luxuriantly and voluptuously celebrates an imagined union with the lover. Dickinson may never have married, but we should not underestimate the power of her imagination or the strength of her passions in the manner of Higginson, who dreaded publishing 'Wild Nights – Wild Nights!' 'lest the malignant read into it more than that virgin recluse ever dreamed of putting there' (in Thomas H. Johnson, ed., *The Poems of Emily Dickinson*, vol. 1, p. 180).

One of the commonest themes in Dickinson's love poetry, however, is not that of fulfilment, but that of loss or renunciation. This is the theme, for example, of 'There came a Day at Summer's full' (322), where the anguish of separation is intensified by the brief union, and of 'I cannot live with You –' (640), where the speaker considers life, death and resurrection in turn, and decides that she could not be with her lover in any of these situations and so they must remain apart. There are two particularly notable aspects of these poems of renunciation. First, they are rarely sentimental. Indeed, Dickinson's poems are never more controlled and spare than here, and as such the form often intensifies the sense of suffering. Secondly, they frequently show some value in renunciation. As Dickinson observes in one **lyric**, 'Renunciation – is a piercing Virtue – / The letting go / A Presence – for an Expectation –' (745). She may have to renounce one thing, but she does this in the expectation of gaining something else. In 'There came a Day at Summer's full' (322), for example, the final stanza contains the hope of reunion after death: there is the possibility that after all the years of suffering and separation the lovers will rise to a 'new Marriage', something even better, more complete than they had, in heaven. Renunciation for Dickinson is not associated with complete self-abnegation, or as Suzanne Juhasz so aptly puts it, for Dickinson, renunciation 'is not about giving up chicken on Sunday so that you might have it on Wednesday. You give up chicken altogether, but you get – maybe ice cream' (*The Undiscovered Continent: Emily Dickinson and the Space of the Mind*, p. 130).

One particularly notable feature of Dickinson's poems about love and marriage is that they frequently draw upon both divine and secular **imagery**. Early critics tended to attempt divisions between the poems on this basis. John Pickard, for example, saw a progression in the love poetry which started with poems about 'the lover's future visit and possible marriage', moved to 'the climactic meeting of the lovers and their resulting separation', and concluded with 'the sublimation of human passion in a celestial marriage as she becomes the Bride of Christ' (*Emily Dickinson: An Introduction and Interpretation*, p. 87). Some critics have considered Dickinson's descriptions of earthly love to stand in for divine love; others have argued her descriptions of divine love suggest earthly love. Today, rather than dividing Dickinson's poems about love and marriage into secular and the divine, critics are more likely to focus upon the way she blends or fuses them. Suzanne Juhasz, for example, sees her 'secular and religious terminology as interdependent ways of representing love' because they can be viewed as 'versions or types of the same experience' (*The Undiscovered Continent*, p. 110). The two types of love seem to become fused in Dickinson's mind.

The language and imagery of divine love appear slightly less frequently in Dickinson's poems about marriage, but still emerge. It is clear in 'Title Divine – is mine!' (1072), but here the 'marriage' so exultantly celebrated is, anyway, not of a conventional, sanctified kind. There is also religious imagery in 'A Wife – at Daybreak I shall be –' (461). The speaker here anticipates with joy her coming transition from 'Maid' to 'Wife'. As she makes her preparations the 'Angels bustle in the Hall'. As she approaches marriage, adulthood, she approaches 'Eternity'; her husband to be is a 'Savior'. The **personas** who speak or are described in such poems as these generally view marriage as an important transitional moment, a rite of passage taking them from being 'girl' to 'woman'. The overall effect of the poems, however, is usually to interrogate the institution of marriage and question its effects upon women as they submit to male authority and lose their status as individuals. 'She rose to His Requirement – dropt' (732), for example, can be seen to emphasise what the woman loses when she takes on 'the honorable Work / Of Woman, and of Wife' (732). What seems to have disturbed Dickinson most was the idea of subordinating the self to another.

NATURE

A number of Dickinson's poems focus upon the relationship between the human and the natural world, a concern she shared with the **Romantic** poets and the **Transcendentalists**. However, as Joanne Feit Diehl argues in *Dickinson and the Romantic Imagination*, 'the Wordsworthian poet's relation to nature is distinguished by his own passivity'; he is the 'responsive yet calm observer'. In contrast, Dickinson is not there to read nature passively; instead she will more aggressively 'either appropriate the landscape by internalising it, or, obversely deny the boundaries between self and nature by ... impressing herself upon the land' (p. 35). The landscape becomes a projection of an internal drama, as in 'There's a certain Slant of light' (258), or a thing of blood and bone and sinew. This is not to say that Dickinson did not appreciate the external beauty of nature or celebrate the natural world. She has a number of spectacular poems about sunsets, for example, including 'How the old Mountains drip with Sunset' (291); when she views nature with the eye of the artist she can approve and admire. Essentially, however, for Dickinson nature was an antagonist, rarely as benign as the Romantics and Transcendentalists sought to believe. She saw it as either completely indifferent, as suggested in such lyrics as 'Apparently with no surprise' (1624), or as actively threatening, as suggested by the snake in 'A narrow Fellow in the Grass' (986). When writing about natural creatures, Dickinson tended to abjure the traditionally popular 'poetic' animals in favour of such 'unpoetic' ones as rats, bats, flies, frogs, worms and spiders. She also challenged the Romantic idea that communion with nature could have some healing power. In 'I dreaded that first Robin, so' (348), for example, nature has no effect upon the inner pain of the speaker save only to increase that pain because of its mindless indifference. The human and natural worlds for Dickinson are totally separate; no interaction between the two, as 'A Bird came down the Walk –' (328) implies, is actually possible.

POEMS OF DEFINITION

A large number of Dickinson's poems cannot be said to be categorised easily in terms of theme. This is because they are what have been termed as 'poems of definition', that is, poems in which Dickinson attempts to define the nature of certain interior experiences which cannot ultimately be defined. James Olney is probably right in suggesting these poems should more correctly be termed 'poems-of-the-impossibility-of-definition' (*The Language(s) of Poetry*, p.52). The attempt at definition in these poems generally proceeds with the speaker trying to find similarities or differences in concrete physical experience for an experience which is interior and abstract, to describe those things which cannot be known through the senses by way of the senses. These poems are **metaphorical**, but while we are given the *vehicle* the nature of the *tenor* often remains unclear (see Imagery). For examples of these so-called 'poems of definition' see "Twas like a Maelstrom' (414), 'It was not Death, for I stood up' (510 – see Extended Commentaries, Text 1), 'I felt a Funeral, in my Brain' (280), 'He Fumbles at your Soul' (315), and 'There's a certain Slant of light' (258). In these, and many other Dickinson poems, there is an 'it' or a 'he' which essentially remains unidentifiable.

LYRICISM

Dickinson writes **lyric** poetry. The lyric can be defined as a poem, usually short, expressing in a personal manner the feelings and thoughts of an individual speaker (not necessarily those of the poet). This is poetry which is neither narrative nor dramatic, although Dickinson does introduce both narrative and dramatic elements at times. 'A Bird came down the Walk –' (328), for example, is a kind of narrative in that it does relate a brief story. The focus of Dickinson's poetry, however, as is true of most lyric poetry, is on the emotions and ideas of a solitary speaker at a particular moment in time.

LANGUAGE & STYLE

Dickinson's style challenged and disrupted the conventions of the time. She may have engaged with the same themes as her contemporaries, but stylistically her poems are strikingly different, their cadences bearing little resemblance to the flowing mellifluous sounds with which her readers were more familiar. Compare some well-known lines from Elizabeth Barrett Browning's *Sonnets from the Portuguese* with lines from Emily Dickinson's '"Why do I love" You, Sir?' (480). Both are writing lyric poetry, but the stylistic differences are striking:

> How do I love thee? Let me count the ways
> I love thee to the depth and breadth and height
> My soul can reach, when feeling out of sight
> For the ends of Being and ideal Grace. (Barrett Browning)

> 'Why do I love' You, Sir?
> Because –
> The Wind does not require the Grass

To answer – Wherefore when He pass
She cannot keep Her place. (Dickinson)

The difference between Dickinson's style and the dominant nineteenth-century style is the result of many factors, some of which are discussed below. Above all, Dickinson's style can best be described as disruptive and challenging. While she draws upon many of the traditional unifying features of poetry such as rhyme, metre, stanzaic form, repetition, parallelism, she also continually undercuts the patterns these might be expected to form.

CAPITALISATION

Dickinson is notably eccentric in her use of capitalisation. Books on rhetoric at the time sometimes called for the use of capitals to provide emphasis, and it is true that the stress provided by capitalisation can be said to draw our attention and give added weight to many of Dickinson's words. It is not always clear, however, *why* some of her capitalised words should be emphasised. Dickinson may also have been influenced by her study of German, in which every noun is capitalised. It is perhaps best not to place too much emphasis on her use of capitalisation, since it is often difficult to tell from Dickinson's handwriting whether or not she meant a word to be capitalised, and in many cases the decision to capitalise has been an editorial one.

PUNCTUATION

Dickinson uses punctuation to disrupt conventional patterns and to create particular **tonal** effects. This is particularly notable in her use of the dash. Nineteenth-century writers tended to use the dash more often than we do today, particularly in informal writing such as letters. Dickinson, however, uses the dash far more frequently and more functionally than most of her contemporaries.

The dash can isolate a word or group of words. This can be seen in the closing lines of 'Wild Nights – Wild Nights! (249), for example: 'Might I but moor – Tonight – / In Thee!' Here the offsetting of 'Tonight' by the dashes intensifies the longing and desire expressed by emphasising that it is now, tonight, that she wants to be with the lover. The dash is used to isolate words in a more complex manner in 'Title Divine – is mine!' (1072). The speaker attempts to define her own particular state of wifehood: she is, for example, 'The Wife – without the Sign!', 'Royal – all but the Crown!', and 'Betrothed – without the swoon'. The speaker defines what she does and does not possess and uses the dash to separate the one from the other.

The dashes can serve to slow down or speed up the rhythm. At the end of 'There's a certain Slant of light' (258), for example, the dashes impose pauses that formally enact the sense of breathless waiting that is being described: ' When it comes, the Landscape listens – / Shadows – hold their breath –'. If you read these lines as though there were no dashes (they were originally removed by her editors) you will see how much is lost. Similarly, the process of slowly freezing to death is re-enacted rhythmically by the way the dashes impose pauses in the final line of 'After great pain, a formal feeling comes –' (341): 'First – Chill – then Stupor – then the letting go.'

Dashes may suggest the stop and start of speech, helping us identify the tone when we recreate the voice of the written text. Look, for example, at the opening of 'A Bird came down the Walk –' (328):

> A Bird came down the Walk –
> He did not know I saw –
> He bit an Angleworm in halves
> And ate the fellow, raw,

The dashes here create the sense of as aside, when the speaker pauses to clarify the situation to the reader, and this contributes to the informal, conversational tone of the poem.

When the dash occurs at the end of a poem, it frequently serves to undermine a sense of **closure**. In 'Because I could not stop for Death –' (712), for example, we are left with the word 'Eternity', followed by a dash. The dash suggests this is not the end, that more lies beyond, exactly what is indicated by the word 'Eternity' itself.

Finally, Dickinson's dashes sometimes contribute towards undermining the potentially relentless sing-song effect of the **common metre** that Dickinson generally uses (see Rhythm & Metre).

Another type of punctuation that Dickinson uses to great effect is the exclamation mark; this appears primarily in her earlier poetry. It can function to emphasise a statement or, if used quite frequently, can convey a sense of spontaneous speech. It can also suggest such tonal qualities as exultation, **irony**, urgency and surprise. Consider the exultation suggested by the exclamations, for example, in the opening lines of 'Title divine – is mine!' (1072), and the boastful delight they convey in 'I taste a liquor never brewed –' (214) when the speaker declares 'I shall but drink the more!'.

RHYTHM & METRE

Most of Dickinson's poems are based on metres adopted and adapted from hymnology; in particular, she frequently uses **common metre**, also called ballad metre, that is, quatrain stanzas consisting of lines alternately of eight and six syllables, rhymed *abab* or, Dickinson's more usual choice, *abcb*. Devoid of irregularities and variations, this metre can easily sound monotonous and banal. Dickinson continually, however, breaks up the regularity of the common metre with her use of dashes, her **slant rhymes** and her use of **enjambment**, thereby avoiding the potentially sing-song effect that the common metre can produce. This sing-song effect is evident in these famous lines from the hymnist Isaac Watts, with whose work Dickinson was particularly familiar, if not exactly fond:

> O God, our help in ages past
> Our hope for years to come,
> Our shelter from the stormy blast,
> And our eternal home.

The rhythm is entirely without irregularity; everything flows smoothly. Compare this with what Dickinson can do with exactly the same metre through an effective use of punctuation in 'I heard a Fly buzz – when I died –':

> I heard a Fly buzz – when I died –
> The Stillness in the Room
> Was like the Stillness in the Air –
> Between the Heaves of Storm –

The halting uncertain effects created here and throughout the poem with the use of the dashes and the slant rhyme tend to undermine all the smoothness and monotony associated with the metre: it would surely be impossible to ignore Dickinson's subversive techniques and impose upon this stanza the 'ti-tum, ti-tum, ti-tum' effect of Watts's **iambs**. Other useful examples of how Dickinson plays with, and sometimes indeed tortures, the common metre, include 'I felt a Funeral, in my Brain' (280). Here the specific metre used conflicts with and jars against the heavy beats Dickinson suggests to imitate the 'Service, like a Drum'. In 'It was not Death, for I stood up' (510), on the other hand, Dickinson first utilises the potentially hypnotic sing-song effect of the common metre in the first stanza, only then to disrupt the metre in stanza four in order to suggest a change in **tone**, a loss of calm peacefulness.

Rhyme

The majority of Dickinson's poems have quite regular rhyme schemes, although since she often uses slant rhyme, the regularity of the rhyme scheme is not always immediately noticeable. Sound effects are usually of great importance in Dickinson's poems. In 'A narrow Fellow in the Grass' (986), for example, we know she is talking about a snake when we hear the repeated sibilant sounds of the first stanza. Dickinson frequently uses **alliteration, consonance** and **assonance** as well as slant and **exact rhyme** to link the various parts of the poem together and both to create and to disrupt patterns of sound. A notable example of the use of rhyme to create links and patterns is found in 'Wild Nights – Wild Nights!' (see Extended Commentaries, Text 3).

Many of her poems reveal a movement away from or towards exact rhyme. 'A narrow Fellow in the Grass' (986) provides a good example of how Dickinson uses rhyme to build towards a moment of climax. In the first stanza, there is little rhyme observable in 'rides' and 'is', and this helps create a casual, conversational tone; in the next three stanzas there is a movement towards slant rhyme, and in the fifth stanza we reach a strong and decisive exact rhyme at the climactic moment when the speaker claims of the snake that he has

> … never met this Fellow
> Attended, or alone,
> Without a tighter breathing
> And Zero at the Bone –

The chilling nature of the meeting described is beautifully captured in the long and exact 'o' sound of the final rhyme, and intensified by the echo of that sound in 'Zero'.

LANGUAGE

Dickinson's poems reveal a highly compressed, compact use of language; she tends to omit any words or phrases that are inessential. In 'Success is counted sweetest' (67), for example, she describes the sounds of triumph bursting onto the 'forbidden ear' of the dying soldier. The reader must fill in the missing words to make sense of this. His ear, of course, is not 'forbidden' in the obvious sense; the phrase is suggestive of the way he, as part of the defeated army, is not entitled to hear the sounds of triumph. She also frequently omits the phrases we expect to find providing explanatory links between statements. A notorious example of this is in 'He fumbles at your Soul' (315) where she provides no explanation of how the final set-off couplet, 'When Winds take Forests in their Paws – / The Universe – is still –', relates to the preceding lines: is it supposed to compare or contrast with the human situation described? Dickinson's compressed language, the deletion of anything extraneous, often increases ambiguity and allows for a multiplicity of meaning.

Dickinson's language is also highly concrete and visual; she conveys to us her abstract ideas and feelings through concrete **images** of people, objects, events, things that we can immediately identify and often visualise. In 'It dropped so low – in my Regard –' (747), for example, the discovery that something once highly valued is not worth her esteem is described in terms of a piece of pottery falling and smashing on the ground. A mental event is conveyed through physical terms.

Dickinson often uses words in surprising, unexpected contexts, in a manner that makes us rethink something with which we might be quite familiar and creates a moment of disturbance, dislocation. In 'There's a certain Slant of light' (258), for example, she describes this slant of light as one that 'oppresses, like the Heft / Of Cathedral Tunes –'. There are two words here that are used in a surprising manner. First, light is described as oppressive. We might more usually think of light as uplifting, but here it 'oppresses'; it is, **paradoxically**, a light that darkens. Strange, perhaps, but she is quite right: there is a kind of light in winter that does this. Second, cathedral tunes are described in terms of 'Heft', a word that Dickinson's original editor changed, with very poor judgement, to 'weight'. Heft is simply not something we associate with cathedral music, not simply because of music, something aural, is being confused with something tactile, an example of Dickinson's use of **synaesthesia**, but also because of the colloquial nature of that word 'Heft'; it seems at odds with the solemnity of religious music. And yet again she is right – the word 'Heft' conveys so much more than the word 'weight' could.

Dickinson's language often suggests the spontaneity of speech. Many of the features of spoken language, which tends to be disjunctive, fragmented, elliptical, to contain more questions, exclamations and pauses than most written language, appear in her poems, which frequently begin with or refer to 'I', another marker of speech. This sense of the spontaneity of speech is offset in Dickinson's poetry by a certain **aphoristic**, **epigrammatic** style. Here the 'I' is replaced by universals; there is an air of finality and solidity about these aphorisms which is, of course, totally undercut by the irregularities and disorder of the more spontaneous, speech-like lines. For an example of how the conversational and the aphoristic are set off against each other, consider the two parts of 'He fumbles at your Soul' (315).

IMAGERY

Dickinson's poems rely heavily upon **metaphor**, that is, a comparison of two different things or ideas made by fusing them together: one thing is described as being another thing. A metaphor has two different parts: the *tenor* is the subject of the metaphoric comparison while the *vehicle* is the metaphoric word which 'carries over' its meaning. An example of these two parts can be found in the opening line of 254: '"Hope" is the thing with feathers –'. 'Hope' here is the tenor, the subject of the comparison, while 'the thing with feathers' (by implication a bird) is the vehicle, the metaphoric word. This example is typical of many of Dickinson's metaphors in the way it links the abstract with the concrete. Most of Dickinson's metaphors, however, are slightly more complex than this; often the tenor, which is usually abstract, remains unstated: this is what is called an *implicit* rather than an *explicit* metaphor. It is, in fact, frequently quite impossible to pin down what that tenor may be. In 'It dropped so low – in my Regard –' (747), for example, it is relatively easy to identify the vehicle used to describe 'It':

> It dropped so low – in my Regard –
> I heard it hit the Ground –
> And go to pieces on the Stones
> At bottom of my Mind –
>
> Yet blamed the Fate that flung it – *less*
> Than I denounced Myself,
> For entertaining Plated Wares
> Upon my Silver Shelf –

The vehicle is a piece of those 'Plated Wares'; we know, however, that this refers to something else, something more abstract; after all, a piece of pottery or china would not smash at the bottom of one's 'Mind'. 'Plated Wares' are being used metaphorically. But what is the tenor here – what is 'It'? Perhaps we can say no more than that it is something or someone that the speaker has highly valued and now realises was not worth her esteem.

At other times the tenors of Dickinson's metaphors are difficult to identify because her images are primarily not comparisons of two objects, but comparisons of feelings with some object. In 'It was not Death, for I stood up' (510), for example, although we are given many concrete comparisons of what 'it' is like and what 'it' is not like, at the end we are still not able to say with much confidence what 'it' is. Here, as in many other of her poems of definition (see Themes, on Poems of Definition), Dickinson attempts to describe a feeling, a psychic experience, with the use of **analogy**, with **simile** and metaphor. The descriptions are so suggestive that we can understand the feelings, even though, like Dickinson herself, we might not be able to put a specific name to them and any paraphrase would become reductive. What Dickinson has to say generally eludes paraphrase; it can really be said only in the manner it is presented to us on the page.

PART FOUR

EXTENDED COMMENTARIES

TEXT 1   IT WAS NOT DEATH, FOR I STOOD UP 1862 (1891)

It was not Death, for I stood up,
And all the Dead, lie down –
It was not Night, for all the Bells
Put out their Tongues, for Noon.

It was not Frost, for on my Flesh
I felt Siroccos – crawl –
Nor Fire – for just my Marble feet
Could keep a Chancel, cool –

And yet, it tasted, like them all,
The Figures I have seen
Set orderly, for Burial,
Reminded me, of mine –

As if my life were shaven,
And fitted to a frame,
And could not breathe without some key,
And 'twas like Midnight, some –

When everything that ticked – has stopped –
And Space stares all around –
Or Grisly frosts – first Autumn morns,
Repeal the Beating Ground –

But, most, like Chaos – Stopless – cool –
Without a Chance, or Spar –
Or even a Report of Land –
To justify – Despair.   (510)

In this poem, the speaker is trying to describe a feeling or experience that
she finds basically indescribable: she can say what it is like and what it is
not, but she cannot specify exactly what it is. In the first two stanzas the
speaker begins trying to define the experience through describing what 'It'

is not: not death, night, frost nor fire. She then moves on to suggest 'It' is nevertheless like all these things, and finally attempts to suggest the effect which 'It' produces. The poem provides a series of possibilities, of alternatives and opposites, but never, however, precisely identifies what 'It' is.

This is an example of one of Emily Dickinson's many so-called poems of definition (see Themes, on Poems of Definition), that is, poems which attempt to define the nature of certain inner mental experiences. These poems are often said to have associations with **riddles**. In such works as 'It was not Death', we are presented with a unidentified 'It', the essence of which the speaker then attempts to capture for us. 'Tell all the Truth but tell it slant –' Dickinson remarks in another lyric (1129): this would appear an accurate description of her own approach in these poems of definition. She tends to proceed through **analogy** and description, finding likenesses or differences to connect the abstract mental feeling or experience with more easily apprehended objects and events in the concrete, physical world. Ultimately, we are usually left with the sense that the feeling or experience cannot be defined, cannot be explained in any other way than the way Dickinson describes it in her poem. Consequently, as James Olney suggests, these poems 'might more exactly be called 'poems-of-the-impossibility-of-definition' (*The Language(s) of Poetry*, p. 52). This analysis will provide an example of how we might approach these difficult and ultimately undefinable poems through a close examination of Dickinson's images.

In 'It was not Death, for I stood up', Dickinson attempts to convey the essence of a basically indescribable experience primarily through **metaphors** of bodily sensation. Something essentially abstract and unknowable is conveyed in as concrete a manner as possible. The problem we find in understanding these metaphors is that part of the metaphor is missing. A metaphor has two different parts: the *tenor* is the subject of the metaphoric comparison while the *vehicle* is the metaphoric word which 'carries over' its meaning. We can find many clear vehicles in 'It was not Death, for I stood up', but what is the tenor? It is simply 'It' – that which Dickinson is trying to describe. The opening stanza offers a series of negatives, focusing on images of death and of light. First there is a visual image: 'It' is not death, since she is standing, 'And all the Dead, lie down'. Then, she moves to the aural. It cannot be night, since the bells are ringing for noon. The speaker is trying to make the feeling as concrete as possible, and here even the idea of the sound of bells is conveyed in an intensely physical manner; it is not simply that they ring: they 'Put out their Tongues, for Noon'. Do you think, however, that the speaker could be revealing some confusion in her mind with this description? After all, is it really possible to distinguish when the bells are tolling noon and when they are tolling midnight? The second stanza, continuing with the negatives, focuses on images of cold and heat, moving away from the visual and aural to the tactile. The idea that it cannot be frost because she feels such heat is effectively conveyed in the image of having Siroccos, hot, oppressive and dusty winds, crawling upon her flesh. Immediately, however, she denies heat. Her 'Marble feet', marble perhaps reminding us of tombstones, are cold enough to keep a Chancel – the part of a church containing the altar – cool. Again, confusion is suggested, for she feels both cold and heat and yet neither.

The intensely concrete and sensually apprehensible way in which Dickinson conveys this abstract feeling or experience is beautifully demonstrated in the way she summarises the condition at the beginning of stanza three. This is not a feeling she conceptually recognises, but something she *tastes*, something she *sensually* recognises. Although it is none of the things she has named so far, 'it tasted, like them all'. She began by claiming this feeling is not death, since she 'stood up' and so intellectually she knows it is not death; however, now she is reminded by her body of bodies set out for burial: she feels like a corpse. Dickinson now moves into a new sequence of analogies in stanza four. A sense of constraint sets in, emphasised by the **anaphoric** lines. She feels her life is 'shaven' and 'fitted to a frame'. What does this suggest about her free will? The image that follows, 'could not breathe without a key', intensifies this by presenting herself as some kind of puppet. The combination of images suggests a self which is restrained and rigid.

Stanza five begins with a horrifying and oppressive sense of nothingness: 'When everything that ticked – has stopped – / And Space stares all around –'. What is it that 'ticked'? It could be the pulse of the universe itself, or of the individual. Why should frosts here be described as 'Grisly'; what do they do to the seeds, the potential for life, that still lies within the ground? She, like the seeds, seems to be placed in a state of suspended animation. And yet, while the seeds may spring to life in the new year, this possibility does not seem open to her; she seems left in this state of eternal suspended animation.

What is particularly horrifying about this experience, the last stanza suggests, is that it is most 'like Chaos'. There is no logical order or progression here. We can see that, formally at least, in her attempt to define the nature of the experience the speaker has been attempting to impose some kind of order. There is, for example, quite an orderly listing, as though logically moving from one point to another, and this listing is emphasised with the use of repetition, particularly with the anaphora of such lines which begin with 'It was not ...' or 'And'. For there to be order and progression, however, there needs to be a point towards which one can progress, and this particular feeling appears 'Stopless'. At least with death there is an end; here there seems to be no relief. It is simply 'most, like Chaos – Stopless – cool – / Without a Chance'. The language and images, at this point, are more abstract, as if the attempt to pin down the experience has been given up as hopeless. But the poem ends with one last attempt, one final concrete analogy. The speaker now seems like a shipwrecked person on a raft, with no 'Spar', nothing to use to create a mast; there is not even the possibility of land 'To justify – Despair'. This final line has been read by some critics as indicating that despair is the feeling she has been attempting to describe. But surely despair is something too passionate, too violent, to describe what she has been feeling, experiencing. What these lines seem to suggest is that there is no hope of land, of anything that lies beyond this suffering, which would justify her feeling even despair: in her condition, despair itself would be meaningless. Perhaps all we can confidently claim is that 'It' is an overwhelming moment of psychic disturbance caused by suffering so intense that the afflicted individual feels emotionally dead: so indifferent, estranged, empty, that she cannot even feel 'Despair'.

TEXT 2   I HEARD A FLY BUZZ – WHEN I DIED –   1862 (1896)

> I heard a Fly buzz – when I died –
> The Stillness in the Room
> Was like the Stillness in the Air –
> Between the Heaves of Storm –

The Eyes around – had wrung them dry –
And Breaths were gathering firm
For that last Onset – when the King
Be witnessed – in the Room –

I willed my Keepsakes – Signed away
What portion of me be
Assignable – and then it was
There interposed a Fly –

With Blue – uncertain stumbling Buzz –
Between the light – and me –
And then the Windows failed – and then
I could not see to see –   (465)

Dickinson thoroughly explores every aspect of death in her poetry. She considers the physical, the psychological and the emotional aspects of this unknowable experience and examines death from the perspective of both the living and the dying. The words of this particular poem are spoken by a person who has died and is recollecting the moment of death. The speaker has made a will; everything assignable has been given away and all that is left is her soul. The room is silent and still, everyone waits in anticipation of some sign, expecting something momentous to happen, expecting to witness the redemption of the soul. And then a trivial ordinary house fly appears, and the speaker's consciousness is extinguished.

Dickinson's fascination with death, as revealed here and in many other poems, may initially appear somewhat strange and unhealthy to the twentieth-century reader, but biographical, historical and cultural readings can make this fascination understandable by placing such poems as this within the social, religious and cultural contexts of her time. In our society, death has become rather a taboo subject, and ignored as much as possible, but as Cynthia Griffin Wolff notes, 'few in Emily Dickinson's world could put death out of mind, for it was too daily and too near' (*Emily Dickinson*, p. 69). There was the constant threat of tuberculosis, smallpox, typhoid, pneumonia which could prove fatal; pregnancy and childbirth were far more dangerous than they are now. There were no antibiotics and surgery would be performed without anaesthesia. Women played a particularly important role as watchers over the dying and this perhaps made them even more conscious of its continual presence in their lives. Dickinson herself participated in many deathbed vigils, and at the age of thirteen was allowed to watch over, and then view, the dead body of her friend Sophia Holland; as Griffin says, this vigil constituted 'a part of Emily Dickinson's training for womanhood in mid-nineteenth-century Amherst' (p. 77).

Deathbed vigils were particularly important to those with religious faith, since this was believed to be the moment when the soul left the body for another world, to meet the redeemer. So, as in this **lyric**, the watchers would gather hoping to see this, to see if any evidence of the afterlife would be provided. The moment of death was of particular interest to Calvinists (see Historical & Literary Background, on The Puritan Heritage), who believed the behaviour of the dying provided an indication of whether or not the soul was saved. If the dying person demonstrated acceptance and died calmly, the soul could be sure of its election; if the dying person struggled against death, he or she was not likely to be destined for heaven. In this lyric, the speaker may pass relatively calmly, but the traditional religious view of death as a peaceful release from the pain of life which provides the reward of immortality is questioned. In this way, Dickinson's poem about death is very different from those produced by most of her contemporaries.

As Barton Levi St Armand has shown (*Emily Dickinson and Her Culture*), Dickinson's poems about death reveal her response to a popular cultural genre of the time: mortuary poetry. Mortuary poetry was in itself part of a larger genre of consolation literature, which included obituary poems, mourner's manuals, and books about heaven. Like many mortuary poems, 'I heard a Fly buzz – when I died –' dwells upon the details of a deathbed scene. But this is mortuary poetry with a difference. A more typical sentimental example can be found in 'The Passing Bell', written by one of Dickinson's contemporaries, Lydia Sigourney, which contains such lines as these:

> To Beauty's shaded room
> The Spoiler's step of gloom,
> Hath darkly stole,
> Her lips are ghastly white
> A film is o'er her sight
> Pray for the soul. (quoted in St Armand, p. 56)

Dickinson is rarely sentimental about death in the manner of Sigourney, who remains conventional in both thought and expression; instead, Dickinson appropriates the paraphernalia of her cultural traditions, but submits them, as St Armand demonstrates, to her techniques of domestication, exaggeration and inversion. One of the ways in which this is done can be seen when we consider the identity of the speaker in this poem. Mortuary poetry, as we would expect, conventionally described the dead or dying from the perspective of the living. Dickinson, however, inverts this in 'I heard a Fly buzz – when I died –'; her first line causes a sense of shock, even dislocation. The use of the dashes to offset 'when I died' create an almost offhand, certainly a detached effect, which seems at odds with the fact that the poem, we must recognise, is spoken by someone who is already dead.

The eyes, traditionally seen as the 'windows to the soul', became a particularly important part of mortuary poetry, both the eyes of the watchers at deathbeds and the eyes of the dying themselves. In 'I heard a Fly Buzz – when I died –', Dickinson plays punningly with the connection between 'I' and 'eye'. The 'I' attempts to maintain calmness and control throughout, but the 'eye/I' nevertheless ultimately fails. The first reference to the interfering fly is made in an offhand manner, and the emphasis is on what is heard rather than what is seen. The speaker is absorbed by the charged atmosphere of the room. How does Dickinson create such a striking sense of intense silence and anticipation? The **simile** which compares the stillness of the room to the stillness of a calm moment in the midst of a storm suggests that the air, although quiet, is charged with possibility: something is about to occur, the room is full of tension. Everyone, including the speaker, is waiting, full of awe, for the moment of death. The focus now moves to the 'Eyes around' which are watching: the onlookers wait breathlessly to see what will occur at the climactic moment of death, when 'the King / Be witnessed – in the Room –'. Moving back to the 'I' who speaks, the dying person gives away her 'Keepsakes', mementoes for those who survive her. She signs away 'What portion of me be / Assignable', reminding us that there is one portion, her soul, over which she has no control. And then 'There interposed a Fly –'. Initially just mentioned as though a minor distraction, the buzz of the fly now takes up the whole field of the speaker's perception. This last stanza begins with a very complex use of **alliteration** and **synaesthesia**. The fly interposes 'with

Blue – uncertain stumbling Buzz'. The repetition of the 'b' and 's' sounds here contribute to the uncertain stumbling which is enacted in the whole progress of the poem. Dickinson may be using the regular rhythms of the **common metre**, but the repeated halting of the rhythm through the use of dashes imposes a sense of awkwardness. The adjective 'stumbling', usually used to describe an action, here also describes a sound, and so does the adjective 'Blue'. How can a sound have a particular colour? As the fly interposes, perception shifts away from the rituals of death to the actuality of death, and the fusion of different sense impressions here effectively evokes that moment when consciousness is about to fail. Noises are intensified; all the senses seem to merge and distort. The fly interposes 'Between the light – and me –'. Is this supposed to mean the light which would lead us to heaven or simply the light from the windows? The **ambiguity** is intensified when 'the Windows failed': is this a reference to the literal windows or the speaker's eyes, those windows to the soul? The poem ends with the complete and final erasure of consciousness and understanding: 'I could not see to see –'. It remains unclear, however, whether the light that is obscured is a divine light or simply the light of day, the light coming through the window.

One answer might be suggested in this poem by Dickinson's use of rhyme. The final words in the second and fourth line of each stanza except the last are **slant rhymes**. In the final stanza we have **exact rhymes**. When a poet does something like this, we need to ask why, to consider if this variation might have some function. Does the exactness of the rhyme at the end perhaps emphasise a sense of finality, suggesting that this is all there is, that there is no afterlife to follow, that the light must have been only the common light of day? Against this, however, we have to put the fact that the poem ends not with a full stop, which might contribute towards emphasising finality, but with a dash, and this dash could be considered to suggest something more, that this is the end, but not the conclusion, that there is something more to follow, that the light may indeed have been a divine one. The ambiguity that results from the conflicting implications of the formal devices of rhyme and punctuation seems to indicate very simply that we are left with no answers. Dickinson, who had an early religious crisis, wanted to believe, but did not possess the confidence of many of her contemporaries that death was followed by resurrection. It was, however, a subject that interested her intensely. In her letters, her repeated questions about the deaths of friends and acquaintances suggest she hoped that some last words or gestures from the dying would overcome her own doubts and confirm the existence of an afterlife. Here, however, she seems to imply this is sentimental wishful thinking. It has even been suggested that the lyric is a grim joke. All expectations are frustrated, **ironically** undermined, by Dickinson's strategies of subversion: the watchers wait for the moment 'when the King / Be witnessed' but all that appears is the insignificant buzzing fly. The fly is a grim reminder of what awaits the body after death: putrefaction, decay; the fly is the only 'King' that we can guarantee we shall meet in death.

TEXT 3   WILD NIGHTS – WILD NIGHTS! 1861 (1891)

Wild Nights – Wild Nights!
Were I with thee
Wild Nights should be
Our luxury!

Futile – the Winds –
To a Heart in port –
Done with the Compass –
Done with the Chart!

Rowing in Eden –
Ah, the Sea!
Might I but moor – Tonight –
In Thee!   (249)

After Dickinson's death, her poems were edited for publication by Mabel Loomis Todd, a family friend, and Thomas Wentworth Higginson, Dickinson's longtime correspondent and literary adviser. This poem eventually appeared in the second selection they published, but Higginson had many reservations: 'One poem only I dread a little to print – that wonderful "Wild Nights", – lest the malignant read into it more than that virgin recluse ever dreamed of putting there' (in Thomas H. Johnson, ed., *The Poems of Emily Dickinson*, vol. 1, p. 180). Higginson surely underestimated the imagination of his 'virgin recluse'. In this luxuriant celebration of an imagined union with a lover, a union which seems to embrace both passionate excess and peaceful contentment, the speaker clearly has in mind exactly what the 'malignant' – and certainly any twentieth-century reader – might see in it. Dickinson wrote many poems about love, and in many different voices; she can be playful, flirtatious, submissive, reverential, exultant, sceptical, and, most notably of all, she can be highly sensuous. This analysis will attempt to demonstrate how metre, rhyme, diction, **imagery** and even punctuation can all be seen to contribute to the creation of tone in 'Wild Nights – Wild Nights!'

'Wild Nights – Wild Nights!': this is quite a theatrical and suggestively erotic opening. In the context of the poem, with its references to compasses, charts and ports, wild nights literally seem to refer to turbulence and storm. Dickinson is conjuring up a stormy nocturnal seascape, the wildness of nature. But Dickinson frequently conflates inner and outer landscapes and there is clearly a **metaphorical** meaning to 'Wild Nights', a suggestion of the wildness of human passion. This first stanza, with its emphatic thrice repeated evocation of 'Wild Nights' and its exclamations, suggests desire and exultation. This is also notable in the dramatic opening **spondees** which brilliantly capture the sense of turbulence and storm. The metre then changes to a regular pattern of **iambic dimeter**, two feet to each line, as the **tone** begins to suggest not only exultation but also a sensuous luxuriating – the word itself is used by Dickinson – in the thought of union with the lover. The sensuousness of the tone here is at least in part the effect of the rhyme which establishes links and patterns throughout the stanza. There is the internal rhyme of the **assonantal** long drawn out 'i' of 'Wild Nights – Wild Nights!', with its suggestion of yearning, and there are the soft drawn out end rhymes of 'thee' and 'be' and 'luxury'. Dickinson rarely uses such insistent rhyme as she does here, where rhyme, either the long 'i' or the long 'e', links together nearly every word in the stanza. And she rarely has three consecutive lines with end rhyme, particularly such **exact rhymes** as here, where we also find, perhaps significantly, the linking of the **masculine** endings of 'thee' and 'be' with the **feminine** ending of 'luxury'. In itself, the insistence of the rhyme should alert us to the fact that the poet is using it to create specific effects. Here, it does two things. First, it creates harmony with its patterning effect. More importantly, however, since the two rhyming sounds are the long 'i' of 'I', and the long 'e' of 'thee' it could also be said to link together the 'I' and the 'thee', effecting formally, that is, the union which is thematically anticipated and desired, but not achieved.

In the second stanza she claims that those wild stormy nights would be a luxury if she were with her lover because she would then be protected from the wildness. She would be like a ship safely in port, no longer needing the guidance of compass and chart: she would be at home. The tone initially seems calmer, more peaceful. The pace is slowed down by the use of dashes; the rhythm becomes more musical, lilting. Almost immediately, however, the exultant tone re-emerges with the **anaphoric** repetition of phrase and the exclamation in the second two lines: 'Done with the Compass – / Done with the Chart!' The emphasis falls heavily on 'Done' here, the effect both of the repetition of the word and the use of the strong stressed syllable at the start of each line. She rejects, dismisses, throws to the winds all compasses and charts: they are no longer required once the speaker is united with the lover. Do you think it is significant, then, that the metre in this stanza is quite irregular? Could Dickinson's rejection of a regular formal pattern in some way reflect or enact her speaker's rejection of all guides, all compasses and charts?

In the third stanza Dickinson returns to the image of sailing: now rowing would be a joy. This is, however, a different kind of sea now, a rejuvenating sea of love that is pleasurable, an Eden or paradise, an idyllic place of perfect harmony. Exultation seems to be replaced by sensuality, as the speaker luxuriates in the imagined pleasures. This tone is particularly notable in the line 'Ah, the Sea!'; the long drawn out vowels here create a much dreamier, more sensual effect than the exultant exclamation of 'Done with the Compass – / Done with the Chart!'. These long drawn out vowels are continued and echoed in such words as 'rowing' 'Eden', 'moor', and 'Thee'. The assonantal rhymes of the first stanza reappear: the 'i', found in the third line, 'Might I but moor – Tonight –' and the 'e', found in 'Eden', 'Sea', and 'Thee'. As the poem ends, the tone manages to combine both exultation and sensuousness: 'Might I but moor – Tonight – / In Thee!' There is emphasis, with the alliterative 'm', but it is soft. There is exclamation, but it is delayed. While the rhythm could have been made more regular by placing 'Tonight' on the final line, its actual position, particularly since it is offset by dashes which create pauses, creates an air of anticipation: the speaker is sensuously putting off that final climactic moment when she thinks of being 'In Thee!'

Do you think this poem is structured around a contrast or a similarity? That is, do you think Dickinson is suggesting that the delight she finds with her lover is the sensuous delight of peace, safety and calm that contrasts with the wildness of a troubled world? Or, is she suggesting that this imagined wildness of nature is similar to, reflects, a human, internal wildness, that the wildness outside is mirrored in their own wild and exultant passions? The two interpretations may, from a logical perspective, contradict each other, but the poem ultimately seems to support both, in much the same way as it ultimately blends the tones of passionate exultation and quiet sensuousness.

PART FIVE

BACKGROUND

EMILY DICKINSON'S LIFE

Emily Elizabeth Dickinson was born on 10 December 1830, in Amherst, Massachusetts, a town with strong Calvinist roots. Her mother, Emily Norcross, came from a prosperous and well-respected family. Her father, Edward Dickinson, was a lawyer, politician and the treasurer of Amherst College. He believed strongly in the importance of education and great care was given to the intellectual development of his children: Austin (1829–95), Emily (1830–86) and Lavinia (1833–99). In 1840 Emily Dickinson was sent to Amherst Academy, a school noted for its enlightened curriculum. Subsequently, she spent a year at Mount Holyoke Female Seminary; here she suffered a serious religious crisis. Waves of religious revivalism were sweeping New England, and at Mount Holyoke students were encouraged to declare their faith openly and publicly. Dickinson was unable to do so. Although drawn towards religious commitment, she could not submit to the doctrines or wholeheartedly accept the beliefs of the orthodox churches. The question of religious faith remained a subject which preoccupied her throughout her life.

Dickinson had a close relationship with her elder brother, Austin, who became a partner in their father's law firm, and with his wife, Sue Gilbert, who had been a schoolmate of Emily's at Amherst Academy. The marriage of Austin and Sue was not a happy one, and problems between them culminated with Austin having an affair with the writer and lecturer Mabel Loomis Todd, a family friend. Dickinson was so devoted to her brother's wife that several critics have concluded that Sue was the real love of her life. Whether Dickinson consciously saw her love for Sue as lesbian in a physical sense or whether it was just a romanticised emotional attachment is much debated by those who subscribe to this view of Dickinson's love life.

Dickinson started writing poetry in her late twenties and after submitting some poetry to the *Atlantic Monthly* began a correspondence with its editor, Colonel Thomas Wentworth Higginson. This lasted twenty years, during which time Dickinson frequently sought his advice on literary matters, although fortunately did not seem to follow it. Dickinson's mother fell ill with an undiagnosed malady in 1855, and the responsibility for her care and all household matters fell to her daughters. From about 1860, Dickinson very gradually began to withdraw from the world. Her father died in June 1874, and a year later her mother became paralysed and remained an invalid, requiring constant attention, until her death in 1882.

Dickinson became increasingly reclusive; in time, even old friends were not accepted as visitors, although she kept up an extensive correspondence and cannot be said, in this sense, to have cut herself off from the world. Her behaviour does not appear to have seemed very odd to her family, even though to outsiders she soon became known as 'the myth'. Why Dickinson decided upon seclusion is not clear; as a young woman, she certainly took an active normal part in Amherst social life. Her decision may have been the result of a combination of factors. It has variously been suggested that she was agoraphobic, that it was part of a pose, a performance, that it was done in order to avoid the social obligations imposed upon nineteenth-century women and allow her time to write, and that she was the victim of disappointed love. This latter explanation was strongly favoured by many early biographers and fuelled by the discovery of a series of letters addressed to an unidentified 'Master'. These elements of her life have been highly romanticised.

Dickinson published only seven of her poems during her lifetime. The remainder she assembled into groups, stitched them up into packets – known as the 'fascicles', and accumulated them in a bureau drawer. Her attitude towards publication was ambivalent. Although she frequently reveals a desire to be known as a poet, to achieve some kind of fame, she seems to have been discouraged from publishing partly by Higginson, who could not understand her new and idiosyncratic style and wanted her to change the poems, and by her acceptance of the nineteenth-century ideology that it was distasteful for a lady to exhibit herself publicly. After Dickinson died of a kidney disease in 1886, a box containing 900 of the poems was found by her sister Lavinia, and the process of publishing Dickinson's works began.

As many early critics placed the emphasis on Dickinson the social recluse when considering her life, so they also tended to claim that her poetry had little or no relation to the historical period in which she lived and that she was as indifferent to the literary movements of her day as she was to its greatest events. Both claims, however, need to be qualified. It would certainly be difficult to tell from her poetry that she lived in an age which saw the beginning of the campaign for women's rights or the campaigns for educational and prison reform and for the abolition of slavery. There is not even any hint in her poetry of the Civil War (1861–5) to which this last campaign ultimately led. It would, nevertheless, be a mistake to claim that Dickinson's work was produced in isolation, and some of the ways in which we can see Dickinson interacting with her historical period and other literary writers are considered below.

THE PURITAN HERITAGE

One of Dickinson's most striking connections with her historical moment is revealed in the influence of her Calvinist or Puritan heritage. Calvinism is the movement of thought and practice following from the work of John Calvin (1509–64). Puritanism, which began as a sixteenth-century movement within English Protestantism to purify religion of all Roman Catholic forms and influences, is one of its stricter expressions, and was brought to New England by the Pilgrim Fathers who settled New England in the seventeenth century. Puritanism held that man was made a pure being, in his Creator's image, but became fallen and corrupted through his wilful turning from the good. Some, known as the Elect, were predestined to salvation; their selection was effected not by any virtue of their own but predestined by God. The Puritan's strong sense of sin and damnation led to a strict pattern of life, and although Puritanism was coming under attack during the mid nineteenth century from new liberal ways of thought, it was still very present, and influential, in Dickinson's Amherst. During her youth, in the midst of what was called the Second Great Awakening, the spirit of revivalism swept New England. At Mount Holyoke Female Seminary, the headmistress Mary Lyon instigated eleven revival campaigns; Dickinson, who spent one year at this school, rebelled against the evangelical fervour, and although repeatedly encouraged to declare herself as a Christian was too full of doubts, too resistant to the doctrines, to declare herself anything but a 'pagan'. While all the other members of her family joined the church, she remained unconverted and so ineligible for church membership. Her Calvinist heritage nevertheless provided her with numerous images and topics for her poetry. More generally, the Bible is one of her main literary influences, particularly Revelation, her favoured source for images. Familiarity with the Bible was an unquestioned part of New England education and it has a primary text in schools. Religious language and imagery, therefore, particularly that drawn from Revelation and from the Calvinist doctrines with which her society was so imbued, can be found throughout her poems. The language and images, however, usually take on new meanings in her poems: she plays with and adapts the doctrines and language for her own ends. Such words as 'Salvation', 'Sacrament', 'Eden', 'Seal', and 'Election' are transformed, redefined, in her hands.

ROMANTICISM & TRANSCENDENTALISM

Romanticism is a literary and philosophical movement dating from 1789, the time of the French Revolution, to about 1830. A number of general characteristics can be seen as loosely characteristic of the English Romantics, a group which includes such poets as Wordsworth, Coleridge, Keats, Shelley and Byron. These characteristics include a valuing of feeling and emotion over reason, an interest in the investigation of the self and a new concern with nature. In America, some of the tenets of Romanticism were appropriated and developed in **Transcendentalism**. The Transcendentalists were a group of writers and thinkers who believed God was immanent in nature and man, that the Soul was present in all things, and that the physical senses needed to be transcended through the truth of intuition. One concern that Dickinson shares with both the Romantics and the Transcendentalists is the relationship between the human and the natural world. Joanne Feit Diehl argues in *Dickinson and the Romantic Imagination* that her view of this relationship, however, was quite different (see Themes, on Nature). For Dickinson nature was often an antagonist, rarely as benign as the Romantics and Transcendentalists sought to believe. She saw it as either completely indifferent, as suggested in such lyrics as 'Apparently with no surprise' (1624), or, sometimes as actively threatening, as suggested by the snake in 'A narrow Fellow in the Grass' (986). The human and natural worlds for Dickinson are totally separate; no interaction between the two, as 'A Bird came down the Walk –' (328) implies, is actually possible. This is not to say that Dickinson did not appreciate the external beauty of nature or celebrate the natural world. Indeed in some respects she can be said to celebrate it, for itself, more than the Romantics or Transcendentalists. While they sought to express the spirit of the world, to rise above the material in order to celebrate what lies beyond, she, in such poems as 'I taste a liquor never brewed –' (214), rejoices in the material world itself: for Dickinson, paradise lies in the here and now.

The most influential Transcendentalist writer of Dickinson's time was Ralph Waldo Emerson (1803–82). 'I taste a liquor never brewed –' (214) has been shown to be a rather tongue-in-cheek version of what Emerson has to say about poetic inspiration in his essay 'The Poet', and certainly undercuts Dickinson's claim to Higginson that 'I … never consciously touch a paint mixed by another person' (Thomas H. Johnson, ed., *The Letters of Emily Dickinson*, p. 415). The main things that attracted Dickinson to Emerson were his emphasis on personal experience over tradition and his belief in self-discipline, self-education, self-reliance, and the potential of the individual soul.

NINETEENTH-CENTURY AMERICAN WOMEN

In opposition to the ideas of self-reliance promoted by the **Transcendentalists** like Emerson was the cult of self-abnegation promoted for women. Women, according to such ideology, were responsible for maintaining moral and spiritual values and for providing a haven from the strife of the world outside the home: their supreme virtues were considered piety, submissiveness, propriety and domesticity. In her letters and poems, Dickinson reveals conflicting attitudes towards this ideology. What seems to have disturbed her most was the idea of subordinating the self to another. In this respect her response compares with her response to religion. Her ambivalence concerning marriage emerges in the conflicting views presented in a series of poems considering the position of the 'wife' (see, for example, 271, 742, 1072).

WOMEN'S WRITING IN THE NINETEENTH CENTURY

Nineteenth-century American women's poetry was widely published in magazines and respected literary journals, and, as Paula Bennett has pointed out, many women poets had a great deal of influence; indeed, she notes, 'one poem by a woman, "The Battle Hymn of the Republic" … can fairly be said to have summed up for many the spirit of the age' (*Emily Dickinson: Woman Poet*, p. 2). Nevertheless, as Bennett observes, few women poets considered themselves to be professionals; those women who wrote for a living were usually prompted to do so by their husband's inability to provide for them. Many warned against the dangers of women striving too hard for fame. Dickinson frequently seems to share the belief that fame and publication were inappropriate for women, but at other times demonstrates a strong desire to be known as a poet. There is clearly some ambivalence, however, in the attitudes of many women writers towards public recognition. Helen Hunt Jackson, for example, like Dickinson born in Amherst and one of her friends and correspondents, had much critical and popular success as a writer. Nevertheless, she preferred to sign her poems 'Anonymous' and wrote about the dangers of fame. On the other hand, she made strenuous attempts to persuade Dickinson to publish, and actually succeeded once, although the poem appeared anonymously.

Most women of the time considered their writing of poetry to be an extension of their domestic lives, and this is reflected in the way it frequently reinforces sentimental domestic ideology. Often conventional in style and thought, this poetry usually focuses on family life, on love and human relationships, on religious faith and on nature. Emily Dickinson may have led an excessively domestic life, but her poetry bears little resemblance to that of such contemporaries as Lydia Sigourney. As she reinscribes domestic ideology in her poems, Sigourney repeatedly confirms her readers' expectations; Dickinson, on the other hand, surprises and challenges them. She may draw upon the same subjects, such as love, death and nature, but she treats these subjects in quite a different manner, questioning, for example, the institution of marriage, challenging traditional religious beliefs, celebrating the sensual material world rather than the spiritual. Another characteristic of much nineteenth-century American women's writing was its concern with reform. Helen Hunt Jackson's novel *Ramona* (1884) and her study *Century of Dishonor* (1881), for example, did much to make the public aware of the plight of the American Indians. Dickinson admired *Ramona* intensely, but only because of the writing, not for the content. Dickinson was simply not a crusader.

The woman poet who Dickinson herself considered to have had the most influence upon her was British: Elizabeth Barrett Browning. In 'I think I was enchanted' (593), Dickinson claims Barrett Browning effected a 'conversion' in her mind; that 'Foreign Lady' taught her the 'Magic' of poetry. Even here, however, it is difficult to see a great deal of similarity in their writing styles, although studies have been done on the similarities between imagery in Dickinson's poem and Barrett Browning's *Aurora Leigh*. Where Dickinson does seem to be most indebted to contemporary women writers, both American and British, is in her choice of plots. As Sandra Gilbert and Susan Gubar have argued, the 'fictional shape Dickinson gave her life was a gothic and romantic one', the mode so frequently employed by other women writers of the time (*The Madwoman in the Attic*, p. 584). As examples of Dickinson's use of the **Gothic**, you could examine 'One need not be a Chamber – to be Haunted' (670), and 'The Soul has Bandaged moments –' (512). While she appropriates such Gothic images as haunted houses and ghosts, and such plots as the heroine besieged by menacing suitors or frightful goblins, as you will notice she does not put the images and plots to conventional use, tending rather to use them to suggest particular states of mind.

PART SIX

CRITICAL HISTORY & FURTHER READING

RECEPTION & EARLY CRITICAL VIEWS

The majority of early responses to Emily Dickinson focused on the apparent strangeness and irregularities of her poetry. Thomas Higginson, one of the editors of the early selections of her work, produced several essays and periodical reviews which attempted to introduce and explain these 'eccentricities': 'when a thought takes one's breath away,' he declared, 'a lesson in grammar seems an impertinence'. The early reviewers, who ranged quite dramatically in their responses, were apparently not always left breathless. An anonymous reviewer in *The Nation* said of the poems that 'in compass of thought, grasp of feeling, and vigor of epithet, they are simply extraordinary' (in Paul J. Ferlazzo, ed., *Critical Essays on Emily Dickinson*, p. 28), while William Dean Howells thought them 'the perfect expression of her ideals' (in Ferlazzo, p. 35). On the other hand, Andrew Lang was annoyed, even affronted, by Dickinson's challenge to conventional rhyme, metre and language. After quoting the lines 'Angels' breathless ballot / Lingers to record thee', he complains, 'This, of course, is mere nonsense. What is a "breathless ballot"? How can a ballot record anything, and how can it "linger" in recording, especially if it is in such a hurry as to be breathless?' (in Ferlazzo, pp. 36–7). By the time the third volume of poems was published by Mabel Loomis Todd in 1896, however, Dickinson's 'eccentricities' were starting to be valued as a sign of her originality and her place in literary history was considered secure. Little, nevertheless, was written about Dickinson for the first decade of the century, and it was only with the appearance of 147 more poems in *The Single Hound* (1914), edited by Dickinson's niece Martha Dickinson Bianchi, that interest again revived. Bianchi did her aunt little service, unfortunately, by writing an introductory essay which began all the speculation about Dickinson's supposed passionate but frustrated attachments. Biographical studies now began to flourish, romanticising Dickinson and focusing upon solving the mystery surrounding the identity of her supposed lover; this mystery has continued to absorb many critics up to the present day. While biographies sensationalised and romanticised Dickinson, critical studies of the time began to see her as an important poet. Now the focus was firmly on her 'originality'. Similarities were noted between Dickinson and the Imagists, and Amy Lowell, one of the most respected **Imagist** poets of the time, included Dickinson in her lectures on this new poetry. Until the mid 1930s, it was such poet-critics as Amy Lowell, Louis Untermeyer, and Conrad Aiken who kept the poetry of Dickinson alive, recognising her, as Paul Ferlazzo observes, to be 'a precursor to the modern spirit' (Ferlazzo, p. 10).

EARLY TWENTIETH-CENTURY CRITICISM

During the 1930s, Dickinson's reputation grew in academic circles as she began to be read by the **New Critics**, with their focus on close textual reading and their de-emphasis on biography. Two significant attempts to reassess the poetry were Yvor Winters's 'Emily Dickinson and the Limits of Judgment' and R.P. Blackmur's 'Emily Dickinson: Notes on Prejudice and Fact'. Both critics are, admittedly, ambivalent in their responses. Winters, for example, thought her a 'poetic genius of the highest order' and yet abhorred her diction and metre and thought all her poems marred by a trace of 'countrified eccentricity'. 'I like to see it lap the Miles', one of the poems he quotes as an example of her 'defects', was, he declared 'abominable' (in Paul J. Ferlazzo, ed., *Critical Essays on Emily Dickinson*, p. 94). Few critical books on Dickinson appeared during the 1940s and 1950s. There was an attempt to read Dickinson in the spirit of Catholic mysticism, a Freudian interpretation which saw a renounced lover as central to Dickinson's life and work, and two critical studies of more significance: Richard Chase's *Emily Dickinson*, and Donald E. Thackrey's *Emily Dickinson's Approach to Poetry*. With the publication of the variorum edition by Johnson in 1955, however, critical interest in Dickinson began to grow, even proliferate. The first notable reading of the poems based on Johnson's edition was Charles R. Anderson's thematic study, *Emily Dickinson's Poetry: Stairway of Surprise*, 1960, still considered to make a substantial contribution to our understanding of Dickinson's work. This was followed by such influential studies as David Porter's *The Art of Emily Dickinson's Early Poetry*, which examines Dickinson's apprenticeship as poet in 300 early poems; Albert J. Gelpi's *Emily Dickinson: The Mind of the Poet*, which considers her engagement with conflicting cultural influences;

and Brita Lindberg-Seyersted's *The Voice of the Poet: Aspects of Style in the Poetry of Emily Dickinson*, which uses linguistics to analyse Dickinson's language.

CONTEMPORARY APPROACHES

During the late 1970s, critics began to read Emily Dickinson's work from a variety of new perspectives. Placing Dickinson in her historical and cultural context has been the concern of many critics. Karl Keller's *The Only Kangaroo Among the Beauty*, for example, focuses on Dickinson's relation with other American poets, while the cultural historian Barton Levi St Armand's interdisciplinary approach in *Emily Dickinson and Her Culture: The Soul's Society* relates Dickinson to such aspects of her culture as mortuary poetry and folk art. Sandra M. Gilbert and Susan Gubar's extensive discussion of Dickinson in *The Madwoman in the Attic* places her more in the context of a British tradition, as does *Dickinson and the Romantic Imagination*, in which Joanne Feit Diehl explores Dickinson's subversion of the tradition of male **Romanticism** established by Wordsworth, Shelley, Keats and Emerson.

Dickinson's language has continued to attract critical interest, particularly from **feminist** critics. Margaret Homans's *Women Writers and Poetic Identity*, for example, analyses Dickinson's exploration of the power and nature of language. Homans's **deconstructive** and feminist approach to Dickinson and her language strategies is acknowledged and extended by Cristanne Miller in *Emily Dickinson: A Poet's Grammar* and by Helen McNeil in her *Emily Dickinson*. Mary Loeffelholz has taken this discussion of Dickinson's language further in *Dickinson and the Boundaries of Feminist Theory* with her **psychoanalytical** study, drawing particularly upon Jacques Lacan and the feminists influenced by his work.

During the last decade, detailed studies have appeared of the more surprising and unusual aspects of Dickinson's work. The most notable example is Suzanne Juhasz, Cristanne Miller and Martha Nell Smith's *Comic Power in Emily Dickinson*, which takes issue with the one-dimensional vision which focuses on the tragic elements of Dickinson's work and brings the comic aspects of her vision to centre stage. If this study reminds us, usefully, of how Dickinson can make us laugh, Daneen Wardrop's *Emily Dickinson's Gothic: Goblin with a Gauge* suggests she makes us afraid, and draws upon such theorists as Hélène Cixous to analyse the **Gothic** impulse in Dickinson's work. One study whose title may initially give us pause is *Dickinson and Audience*, a collection of essays edited by Martin Orzeck & Robert Weisbuch. Dickinson may have once told Higginson the notion of publication was more foreign to her than 'Firmament to Fin' (in Orzeck & Weisbuch, p. 1), but there is still, as this collection demonstrates, much to be said about her theoretical, her epistolary, and her public and historical sense of an audience.

WORKS CITED

Charles R. Anderson, *Emily Dickinson's Poetry: Stairway of Surprise*, Holt, Rinehart, & Winston, 1960
> A thematic approach to the poems, focusing on art, nature, the inner world, death and immortality, and still considered a useful study of Dickinson

Richard Chase, *Emily Dickinson* , William Sloane, 1951
> Early critical study that has generally been superseded

Joanne Feit Diehl, *Dickinson and the Romantic Imagination*, Princeton University Press, 1981
> Considers Dickinson's subversion of the tradition established by such male **Romantic** poets as Wordsworth, Shelley, Keats and Emerson

Paul J. Ferlazzo, ed., *Critical Essays on Emily Dickinson*, G.K. Hall, 1984
> Useful collection of important essays on Dickinson which also includes many early reviews of the poetry

Albert J. Gelpi, *Emily Dickinson: The Mind of the Poet*, Harvard University Press, 1966
> Early study which considers her engagement with conflicting cultural influences

Sandra M. Gilbert and Susan Gubar, *The Madwoman in the Attic*, Yale University Press, 1979
> Places Dickinson in the context of a British tradition and discusses poetry as performance with an emphasis on the roles Dickinson assumed

WORKS CITED continued

Margaret Homans, *Women Writers and Poetic Identity*, Princeton University Press, 1980
>
> A deconstructive and feminist analysis of issues of nature and the power of language

Suzanne Juhasz, Cristanne Miller and Martha Nell Smith, *Comic Power in Emily Dickinson*, University of Texas Press, 1993
>
> Takes issue with the one-dimensional vision which focuses on the tragic elements of Dickinson's work and brings the comic aspects of her vision to centre stage: an illuminating study and a good read

Karl Keller, *The Only Kangaroo Among the Beauty: Emily Dickinson and America*, Johns Hopkins University Press, 1979
>
> Focuses on Dickinson's relation with other American writers, including Beecher Stowe, Emerson and Whitman

Brita Lindberg-Seyersted, *Voice of the Poet: Aspects of Style in the Poetry of Emily Dickinson*, Harvard University Press, 1968
>
> Draws on linguistic theory to analyse Dickinson's language: still useful but in many ways superseded by recent **feminist** work on Dickinson's language

Mary Loeffelholz, *Dickinson and the Boundaries of Feminist Theory*, University of Illinois Press, 1991
>
> A **psychoanalytical** approach which focuses on the language and draws particularly upon Jacques Lacan and the feminists influenced by his work

Helen McNeil, *Emily Dickinson*, Virago, 1986
>
> Focuses on Dickinson's language and intellectual concerns: feminist and **deconstructive** approach

Cristanne Miller, *Emily Dickinson: A Poet's Grammar*, Harvard University Press, 1987
>
> Draws upon a blend of linguistic, structural, historical and **biographical** analysis to understand Dickinson's language strategies

Martin Orzeck and Robert Weisbuch, eds, *Dickinson and Audience*, University of Michigan Press, 1996
>
> A collection of essays which explores Dickinson's theoretical, epistolary, and public and historical sense of an audience

David Porter, *The Art of Emily Dickinson's Early Poetry*, Harvard University Press, 1966

Early study which examines Dickinson's apprenticeship as poet in 300 early poems

Barton Levi St Armand, *Emily Dickinson and Her Culture: The Soul's Society*, Cambridge University Press, 1984

Contextualises Dickinson by placing her in relation to such aspects of her culture as mortuary poetry and folk art: useful and interesting background reading

Donald E. Thackrey, *Emily Dickinson's Approach to Poetry*, University of Nebraska Press, 1954

Early critical study which has been superseded

Daneen Wardrop, *Emily Dickinson's Gothic: Goblin with a Gauge*, University of Iowa Press, 1996

Draws upon such theorists as Hélène Cixous to analyse the **Gothic** impulse in Dickinson's work

FURTHER READING

Caesar R. Blake and Carlton F. Wells, eds, *The Recognition of Emily Dickinson*, University of Michigan Press, 1968

A collection of early articles on Dickinson which also includes early reviews

Sharon Cameron, *Lyric Time: Dickinson and the Limits of Genre*, Johns Hopkins University Press, 1979

Focuses on the language with reference to issues of temporality in the poetry

Paul Crumbley, *Inflections of the Pen. Dash and Voice in Emily Dickinson*, Lexington, University Press of Kentucky, 1997

Considers the use of the dash in a selection of key poems, in the context of the literary culture of Dickinson's day, and in her letters

Judith Farr, ed., *Emily Dickinson: A Collection of Critical Essays*, Prentice Hall, 1996

A good collection of some of the most important writings on Dickinson

Paul J. Ferlazzo, *Emily Dickinson*, Twayne, 1976

Helpful introductory study

Suzanne Juhasz, *The Undiscovered Continent: Emily Dickinson and the Space of the Mind*, Indiana University Press, 1983
    Argues that living in the mind was a positive solution to the problem of being a poet for Dickinson

Suzanne Juhasz, ed., *Feminist Critics Read Emily Dickinson*, Indiana University Press, 1983
    A useful selection of recent criticism from various feminist perspectives

James Olney, *The Language(s) of Poetry: Walt Whitman, Emily Dickinson, Gerard Manley Hopkins*, University of Georgia Press, 1993
    A study of rhythm, images and language of the three poets

Rebecca Patterson, *Emily Dickinson's Imagery*, University of Massachusetts Press, 1979
    Analyses the **imagery** with specific focus on its eroticism

Elizabeth Phillips, *Emily Dickinson: Personae and Performance*, Pennsylvania State University Press, 1988
    Explores the way Dickinson dramatised herself and the lives of others in her poetry: emphasis on **persona**

John B Pickard, *Emily Dickinson: An Introduction and Interpretation*, Holt, 1967
    Early but still useful introduction to the poetry

Richard B. Sewall, *Life of Emily Dickinson*, 2 vols, Farrar/Faber & Faber, 1974
    Excellent biography, describing Dickinson's life, her family history, and her society and culture

Cynthia Griffin Wolff, *Emily Dickinson*, Knopf, 1986
    Biographical study with critical analyses of the poems

World events	Author's life	Literary events
1826 First crossing of Atlantic under steam		
	1829 Emily's brother, Austin, born	
1830 Death of George IV; accession of William IV	**1830 Emily Elizabeth Dickinson** born at Amherst, Massachusetts	
	1833 Emily's sister, Lavinia, born	**1833-4** On a trip to Europe, Ralph Waldo Emerson meets Carlyle, Coleridge and Wordsworth
		1834 Coleridge dies
		1836 Transcendental Club meets at Emerson's house; Emerson's essay, *Nature,* explains Transcendentalism
1837 Death of William IV; accession of Queen Victoria; Morse invents telegraph		
1839-42 Britain at war with China (Opium Wars)		
	1840 Emily attends Amherst Academy	**1840-2** Margaret Fuller edits Transcendentalist journal, *The Dial*
1843 Bronson Alcott, leading exponent of Transcendentalism, helps found cooperative vegetarian community, 'Fruitlands'		
1845-50 Irish potato famine		**1845** Edgar Allan Poe, *The Raven and Other Poems*
	1847-8 At Mount Holyoke Female Seminary Emily undergoes religious crisis	

World events	Author's life	Literary events
1848 Revolutions in Paris, Berlin, Vienna, Venice, Rome, Milan, Naples, Prague and Budapest; Gold Rush begins in California		**1848** Pre-Raphaelite Brotherhood founded
		1850 William Wordsworth dies; Nathaniel Hawthorne, *The Scarlet Letter;* Margaret Fuller with husband and baby drown in shipwreck
		1854 Henry David Thoreau, Transcendentalist, *Walden*
	1855 Mother falls ill and Emily nurses her	**1855** Walt Whitman, *Leaves of Grass;* Alfred Lord Tennyson, *Maud and Other Poems*
		1857 Elizabeth Barrett Browning, *Aurora Leigh;* Charles Baudelaire, *Les Fleurs du Mal*
	1858 onwards Assembles poems in packets of 'fascicles'	
		1859 Harriet Beecher Stowe, *Uncle Tom's Cabin*
	1860 Begins to withdraw from world	
1861 American Civil War begins; Singer manufactures sewing machine		
	1862 Sends first poems to Higginson at *Atlantic Monthly*	
1863 Abolition of slavery proclaimed, USA		
1865 Surrender of Confederates under General Lee ends American Civil War; Abraham Lincoln, first American President, assassinated		
1866 Ku Klux Klan founded in Southern States		**1866** Algernon Charles Swinburne, *Poems and Ballads*

World events	Author's life	Literary events
1867 USA buys Alaska from Russia		**1868-9** Louisa Alcott, daughter of Bronson, *Little Women*
1869 First transcontinental American railway completed		**1869** Tennyson, *The Holy Grail and Other Poems*
1870-1 Franco-Prussian War		
		1872 Horace Greely (of Amherst), champion of women's rights, black suffrage, pacifism, dies
1873 Inventions of typewriter and barbed wire, USA		
	1874 Father dies	
	1875 Mother becomes paralysed and invalid	
1876 Battle of Little Big Horn		**1876** Stephane Mallarmé, *L'Après-midi d'un Faune*
		1877 Coventry Patmore, *The Unknown Eros and Other Poems*
		1881 Thomas Carlyle dies
	1882 Mother dies	
		1883 George Meredith, *Poems and Lyrics of the Joy of Earth*
		1884 Helen Hunt Jackson, *Ramona*
	1886 Dies of kidney disease, leaving some 900 unpublished poems	
	1890 Her poems 'edited' by Mabel Loomis Todd and T.W. Higginson are published	
	1894 Her correspondence published	
	1954 Her complete poems, edited by T.H. Johnson, published	

alliteration a sequence of repeated consonantal sounds in a stretch of language. The matching consonants are usually at the beginning of words or stressed syllables. This is exemplified by the alliterative 's' in these two opening lines: 'Success is counted sweetest / By those who ne'er succeed' (67)

ambiguity the capacity of words and sentences to have double, multiple, or uncertain meanings. Many of Dickinson's poems as a whole remain ambiguous; there are, for example, many so-called poems of definition in which an attempt is made to define or describe an unspecified 'it', the meaning of which ultimately remains ambiguous

analogy a literary parallel: a word, thing, idea, or story, chosen for the purpose of comparison. In 'He fumbles at your Soul' (315), Dickinson makes an analogy between the way the unidentified 'He' works upon the soul and the way someone plays a piano

anaphora a rhetorical device in which a word or phrase is repeated in several successive clauses. Dickinson uses anaphora in 'It was not Death, for I stood up' (510), when she repeats the phrase 'It was not' at the beginning of various lines, and when she opens her lines repeatedly with 'And' in stanza four

aphorism a generally accepted principle or truth expressed in a short, pithy manner. Dickinson's lines sometimes have an aphoristic quality, but they generally surprise rather than confirm the unexpected. An example can be found in the opening lines of 'Success is counted sweetest / by those who ne'er succeed' (67)

assonance the correspondence, or near-correspondence, in the stressed vowel of two or more words. The long repeated 'o' sound in the final stanza of 'A narrow Fellow in the Grass' (986) provides an example of assonance with the words 'Fellow', 'alone', 'Zero', and 'Bone'

biographical criticism this approach to literature, which interprets a work in terms of the author's life and development of ideas, has been out of fashion since the New Criticism

caesura a pause within a line of verse; Dickinson uses emphatic caesura in 'Title Divine – is Mine!' (1072), the pause being emphasised by the dash

closure the impression of completeness and finality achieved by the ending of some literary works

common metre the metre used in hymns and ballads: quatrain stanzas consisting of lines alternately of eight and six syllables, rhymed *abab* or *abcb*. This is the metre Dickinson most frequently uses

consonance repeated arrangement of consonants, with a change in the vowel that separates them, e.g. flip-flap

couplet a pair of rhymed lines, of any metre. Dickinson rarely uses couplets, but they do appear in some poems: 'Title divine – is mine! / The Wife – without the Sign!' (1072)

deconstructive criticism a radical movement, based on the work of Jacques Derida which holds that all notions of absolute meaning in language are wrong

dramatic monologue a particular kind of lyric poem in which a single character, not necessarily the poet, is speaking. The form was developed in the nineteenth century primarily by Tennyson and Browning

end stopped the end of a line of verse coincides with an essential grammatical pause usually signalled by punctuation. In the following example, the lines are end stopped: 'There's a certain Slant of light, / Winter afternoons –' (258). Compare end stopped with enjambment

enjambment running over the sense and grammatical structure from one verse line or couplet to the next without a punctuated pause, e.g., 'That oppresses, like the Heft / Of Cathedral Tunes' (258) Compare enjambment with end stopped

epigram originally an inscription on a monument; now any short poem which has a sharp turn of thought or point

feminine rhyme rhymed words of two or more syllables, when the last syllable is not stressed; for example, finding / grinding

feminist criticism one of the main tenets of feminist thought is that male ways of perceiving and ordering are inscribed into the prevailing ideology of society and into language itself. Many feminist critics argue that patriarchal culture is marked by the urge to define, categorise and control, and that it subjects thought to binary systems of irreconcilable opposites. Femininity is considered a construction of society and of language. Sexual identity, that we are born with, is distinguished from gender, which would include those traits we are assigned and those traits we are encouraged to acquire

foot, feet in order to work out the metre of a line of verse, it is necessary to divide it into 'feet' which are certain fixed combinations of stressed and unstressed syllables. The main feet are the **iamb** (-/), the **trochee** (/-), the **anapaest** (—/) and the **dactyl** (/—). 'Because I could not stop for Death' (712) is a line of **iambic tetrameter**, while **iambic dimeter** has two feet, e.g. 'A word is dead', and **iambic trimeter** three, e.g. 'A Bird came down the Walk' (328)

Gothic the Gothic novel as it developed at the end of the eighteenth century tends to deal with cruel passions and supernatural terrors, often in a medieval setting or in some exotic world that would have been quite unfamiliar to the readers. Classic examples include Ann Radcliffe's *The Mysteries of Udolpho* (1794) and Matthew Lewis's *The Monk* (1796). More generally, any work concentrating on the bizarre, the macabre, or aberrant psychological states may be called Gothic. Dickinson draws upon classic Gothic plots and uses Gothic images in such poems as 'One need not be a Chamber – to be Haunted –' (670)

image, imagery in its narrowest sense a word-picture, a description of some visible scene or object. More commonly, imagery refers to the figurative language, such as metaphors and similes, in a literary work, or to words which refer to objects and qualities which appeal to the senses and feelings

Imagism a movement in poetry in England and America initiated by Ezra Pound and T.E. Hulme in about 1912. Pound defined an 'Image' as 'that which presents an intellectual and emotional complex in an instant of time'. He described the aims of Imagism as direct treatment of the 'thing' whether subjective or objective; to use no word that does not contribute to the presentation; to compose in the sequence of the musical phrase, not in sequence of a metronome. Critics of the early part of this century, including the Imagist poet Amy Lowell, saw many similarities between the work of Dickinson and the Imagists

irony in general terms, saying one thing while you mean another

lyric a poem, usually short, expressing in a personal manner the feelings and thoughts of an individual speaker (not necessarily those of the poet). Dickinson is a lyric poet

masculine rhyme monosyllable rhyme on the final stressed syllables of lines of verse; for example: wall / fall

metaphor goes further than a comparison between two different ideas or things by fusing them together. A metaphor has two different parts: the *tenor* is the subject of the metaphoric comparison, while the *vehicle* is the metaphoric word which 'carries over' its meaning. An example of these two parts can be found in the opening line '"Hope" is the thing with feathers –' (254). 'Hope' here is the tenor, the subject of the comparison, while 'the thing with feathers' (by implication a bird) is the vehicle, the metaphoric word. Dickinson's metaphors are more often *implicit* rather than *explicit*, and it is frequently difficult to determine exactly what the tenor is.

metonymy a figure of speech: the substitution of the name of a thing by the name of an attribute of it, or something closely associated with it, for example, the 'Crown' for the monarchy. In 'Success is counted sweetest' (67), Dickinson metonymically describes victory in battle as 'taking the Flag'

metre verse is distinguished from prose because it contains some linguistic element which is repeated, creating a sense of pattern. In English verse the commonest pattern is stress- or accent-based metre, which consists of the regular arrangement of strong stresses in a stretch of language. Dickinson most often uses the ballad or common metre associated with hymns

New Criticism a major critical movement of the 1930s and 1940s in the US. The new critics argued for the autonomy of literature, studied in isolation from its biographical and historical context. They saw the work as a linguistic structure in which all the parts are held together as an organic whole; their emphasis was on form and structure

onomatopoeic words which sound like the noise they describe. Dickinson creates an onomatopoeic effect in 'I like to see it lap the Miles' (585) with her choice of consonants in the first few lines; reading these lines out loud will emphasise the locomotive sound produced by l-k-l-p-l-k

oxymoron a figure of speech in which contradictory terms are brought together in what is at first sight an impossible combination: 'darkness visible'

paradox an apparently self-contradictory statement, or one that seems in conflict with all logic and opinion; yet lying behind the superficial absurdity is a meaning or truth. In 'There's a certain Slant of light' (258), for example, winter light is shown to darken the soul; a light which darkens is paradoxical

parody an imitation of a specific work or style in order to ridicule it

pathetic fallacy the equation of your own mood and the world around you: if you are sad, for example, the weather is gloomy. Dickinson might be said to use pathetic fallacy in the last stanza of 'There's a certain Slant of light' (258) when she projects her speaker's feelings upon the landscape

patriarchy a social and political system which gives power and prestige to men, and likely to be regarded by men as the natural order of things

persona the speaker in a poem or other literary work who is clearly not the author. Since the New Criticism, many critics prefer to use 'persona' to designate the speaker even in works which might seem explicitly autobiographical. In 'A narrow Fellow in the Grass' (986), the speaker, who remembers being 'a Boy', is clearly not Emily Dickinson. However, it would probably be misleading to identify any of her speakers as the poet herself

personification a variety of figurative or metaphorical language in which things or ideas are treated as if they were human beings. Dickinson personifies death as a gentleman caller in 'Because I could not stop for Death – ' (712)

psychoanalytical criticism Freud developed the theory of psychoanalysis as a means of curing neuroses in his patients; its concepts have been expanded as a means of understanding human behaviour and culture generally

rhyme consists of chiming or matching sounds at the ends of lines of poetry to create an audible sense of pattern. The rhyme may be **exact** as in 'Title divine – is mine! / The Wife – without the Sign!' (1072) or **slant**, that is inexact or imperfect as when Dickinson rhymes 'Pearl' with 'Alcohol' in stanza one of 'I taste a liquor never brewed –' (214). See also feminine rhymes and masculine rhymes

riddle a deliberately puzzling way of referring to an object or idea. The Sphinx's riddle solved by Oedipus in the Greek legend is typical: what goes on four legs in the morning, two legs at noon and three legs in the evening? (answer: a human being in the three stages of life). Many of Dickinson's poems have associations with the riddle. 'I like to see it lap the Miles' (585), for example, never mentions the word locomotive; we are encouraged to guess what is being referred to on the evidence of the language and descriptions

Romantic movement a European literary movement of the late eighteenth and early nineteenth century which valued feeling and emotion over reason, was interested in the investigation of the self and expressed a new concern for nature

simile a species of metaphorical writing in which one thing is said to be like another and the comparison is made with the use of 'like' or 'as'. 'Come slowly –

Eden' (211) is based around the simile which compares the speaker sipping at Eden with the bee taking nectar from the flower

spondee a metrical foot consisting of two long syllables or two strong stresses. Dickinson begins with a spondee in 'Wild Nights – Wild Nights!' (249)

stanza a unit of several lines of verse

synaesthesia the description of a sense impression in terms more appropriate to a different sense; the mixing of sense impressions in order to create a particular kind of metaphor. In 'There's a certain Slant of light' (258) Dickinson describes winter light as oppressive 'like the Heft / Of Cathedral Tunes'. The visual image of light merges with the tactile image of weight and the aural image of cathedral music

synecdoche a figure of speech in which a part is used to describe the whole of something; for example 'All hands on deck', where 'hands' refers to the sailors

tetrameter in prosody a line of four feet

tone in conveying tone, words can suggest the sense of a particular manner or mood in which a passage should be read

Transcendentalism modes of thought which emphasise the intuitive and mystical powers of the mind, and the possibility of some higher world or realm of existence beyond the world of the senses. More particularly, the Transcendentalists were a group of American writers and thinkers in the early nineteenth century who believed God was immanent in nature and man, that the Soul was present in all things, and that the physical senses needed to be transcended through the truth of intuition. Emerson and Thoreau were members of the group

trimeter in prosody a line of three feet

AUTHOR OF THIS NOTE

Glennis Byron is Senior Lecturer in English Studies at the University of Stirling. She has written and edited various books on nineteenth-century poetry and on Gothic literature, and is the author of the York Notes Advanced on *Frankenstein* and Keats.

NOTES

NOTES

Chinua Achebe
Things Fall Apart

Edward Albee
Who's Afraid of Virginia Woolf?

Margaret Atwood
Cat's Eye

Jane Austen
Emma

Jane Austen
Northanger Abbey

Jane Austen
Sense and Sensibility

Samuel Beckett
Waiting for Godot

Robert Browning
Selected Poems

Robert Burns
Selected Poems

Angela Carter
Nights at the Circus

Geoffrey Chaucer
The Merchant's Tale

Geoffrey Chaucer
The Miller's Tale

Geoffrey Chaucer
The Nun's Priest's Tale

Samuel Taylor Coleridge
Selected Poems

Daniel Defoe
Moll Flanders

Daniel Defoe
Robinson Crusoe

Charles Dickens
Bleak House

Charles Dickens
Hard Times

Emily Dickinson
Selected Poems

Carol Ann Duffy
Selected Poems

George Eliot
Middlemarch

T.S. Eliot
The Waste Land

T.S. Eliot
Selected Poems

Henry Fielding
Joseph Andrews

E.M. Forster
Howards End

John Fowles
The French Lieutenant's Woman

Robert Frost
Selected Poems

Elizabeth Gaskell
North and South

Stella Gibbons
Cold Comfort Farm

Graham Greene
Brighton Rock

Thomas Hardy
Jude the Obscure

Thomas Hardy
Selected Poems

Joseph Heller
Catch-22

Homer
The Iliad

Homer
The Odyssey

Gerard Manley Hopkins
Selected Poems

Aldous Huxley
Brave New World

Kazuo Ishiguro
The Remains of the Day

Ben Jonson
The Alchemist

Ben Jonson
Volpone

James Joyce
A Portrait of the Artist as a Young Man

Philip Larkin
Selected Poems

D.H. Lawrence
The Rainbow

D.H. Lawrence
Selected Stories

D.H. Lawrence
Sons and Lovers

D.H. Lawrence
Women in Love

John Milton
Paradise Lost Bks I & II

John Milton
Paradise Lost Bks IV & IX

Thomas More
Utopia

Sean O'Casey
Juno and the Paycock

George Orwell
Nineteen Eighty-four

John Osborne
Look Back in Anger

Wilfred Owen
Selected Poems

Sylvia Plath
Selected Poems

Alexander Pope
Rape of the Lock and other poems

Ruth Prawer Jhabvala
Heat and Dust

Jean Rhys
Wide Sargasso Sea

William Shakespeare
As You Like It

William Shakespeare
Coriolanus

William Shakespeare
Henry IV Pt 1

William Shakespeare
Henry V

William Shakespeare
Julius Caesar

William Shakespeare
Macbeth

William Shakespeare
Measure for Measure

William Shakespeare
A Midsummer Night's Dream

William Shakespeare
Richard II

William Shakespeare
Richard III

William Shakespeare
Sonnets

William Shakespeare
The Taming of the Shrew

William Shakespeare
Twelfth Night

William Shakespeare
The Winter's Tale

George Bernard Shaw
Arms and the Man

George Bernard Shaw
Saint Joan

Muriel Spark
The Prime of Miss Jean Brodie

John Steinbeck
The Grapes of Wrath

John Steinbeck
The Pearl

Tom Stoppard
Arcadia

Tom Stoppard
*Rosencrantz and Guildenstern
are Dead*

Jonathan Swift
*Gulliver's Travels and The
Modest Proposal*

Alfred, Lord Tennyson
Selected Poems

W.M. Thackeray
Vanity Fair

Virgil
The Aeneid

Edith Wharton
The Age of Innocence

Tennessee Williams
Cat on a Hot Tin Roof

Tennessee Williams
The Glass Menagerie

Virginia Woolf
Mrs Dalloway

Virginia Woolf
To the Lighthouse

William Wordsworth
Selected Poems

Metaphysical Poets

York Notes Advanced

Margaret Atwood
The Handmaid's Tale

Jane Austen
Mansfield Park

Jane Austen
Persuasion

Jane Austen
Pride and Prejudice

Alan Bennett
Talking Heads

William Blake
Songs of Innocence and of Experience

Charlotte Brontë
Jane Eyre

Emily Brontë
Wuthering Heights

Geoffrey Chaucer
The Franklin's Tale

Geoffrey Chaucer
General Prologue to the Canterbury Tales

Geoffrey Chaucer
The Wife of Bath's Prologue and Tale

Joseph Conrad
Heart of Darkness

Charles Dickens
Great Expectations

John Donne
Selected Poems

George Eliot
The Mill on the Floss

F. Scott Fitzgerald
The Great Gatsby

E.M. Forster
A Passage to India

Brian Friel
Translations

Thomas Hardy
The Mayor of Casterbridge

Thomas Hardy
Tess of the d'Urbervilles

Seamus Heaney
Selected Poems from Opened Ground

Nathaniel Hawthorne
The Scarlet Letter

James Joyce
Dubliners

John Keats
Selected Poems

Christopher Marlowe
Doctor Faustus

Arthur Miller
Death of a Salesman

Toni Morrison
Beloved

William Shakespeare
Antony and Cleopatra

William Shakespeare
As You Like It

William Shakespeare
Hamlet

William Shakespeare
King Lear

William Shakespeare
Measure for Measure

William Shakespeare
The Merchant of Venice

William Shakespeare
Much Ado About Nothing

William Shakespeare
Othello

William Shakespeare
Romeo and Juliet

William Shakespeare
The Tempest

William Shakespeare
The Winter's Tale

Mary Shelley
Frankenstein

Alice Walker
The Color Purple

Oscar Wilde
The Importance of Being Earnest

Tennessee Williams
A Streetcar Named Desire

John Webster
The Duchess of Malfi

W.B. Yeats
Selected Poems